AMERICA
AND ITS
FUTURE

A BOOK ON AMERICAN ECONOMIC POSSIBILITIES

FREDERICK L. IMPERIAL

ISBN: 145363231X
ISBN-13: 9781453632314

"Printed by CreateSpace"
eStore link: www.createspace.com/ 3461454

TABLE OF CONTENTS

DEDICATION

To my wife and children

CHAPTER 1

CURRENT ECONOMIC & POLITICAL ISSUES

The near collapse of the financial sector, due mainly to speculation in the real estate markets and excessive risk-taking on Wall Street, has brought America into a very deep and lasting recession.

The response by many Americans these days to the economic and political issues facing them seems to be angst. Despite the many Internets, TV and newspaper articles about real estate and derivatives issues, most people are still in the dark as to what derivatives really are all about.

Can this fiasco happen again and again? How much risks do these financial instruments really present to everyday Americans? The banks were bailed out by the government when they were on the brink of bankruptcy. The government declared that the risks taken by the banks were so excessive that their bankruptcy might bring down the whole American economic system.

In reality, the present total losses of Wall Street total a little over $1 trillion. [1] It is not just the wage earner, as taxpayer, who is footing the bill for those losses; the entire population is negatively affected—enterprise, domestic markets, and government. Government power to ensure more than adequate security is dependent on the economic power of its country. Economic power is central to security, defense, and military power.

The American people, as workers, business or political leaders, taxpayers, and investors, will have to pay a price for this fiasco. We will also have to pay the price for the economic imbalances. Economic stress on the population will bring about related negative social issues such as obesity and high health care costs, drugs and addictions, teenage violence, and others. The government debt and deficits also limit their power to provide the required political, economic, and physical security without negatively impacting productive jobs and the economy. Excessive government debt will mean higher taxes. If government spending results in deficits due to operating expenses rather than investment spending, it will mean an increase in the already excessive debt. Investment spending can be recovered but government operating expenses cannot.

It is fundamentally understood in the field of economics that the more you spend on "guns," the less "butter" the economy can provide. Simply trying to increase the money supply in this situation will bring inflation, meaning a fall in real income for the wage earner from the loss of purchasing power. Excessive respect for the "successful" moneyed people on Wall Street, as well as for the mathematical geniuses they hired to make complex mathematical models to evaluate the risks of return and liquidity of securities, led to this sobering present day economic situation.

I wonder sometimes what happened to that old American belief in the individual. Today, excessive trust in leaders and their supposed technical, economic, and financial theories and applications seems to override common sense. As an example, even in the distressing present financial and economic situation, the word from economists and investors is that hope for recovery lies in greater consumer spending. There are millions of unemployed, underemployed, homeless, and people going hungry. Costs of many goods and services are still rising (metals, some foods, some imports) due to the depreciation of our currency, continuing wage reductions, and even layoffs by local governments such as those in Nevada and California. The personal savings rate in the country, as of 2009, had only gone up to a little over 4.1 percent of national income. [2] Government is expecting over $1.5 trillion in budget deficits for the 2010–11 fiscal years, [3] and economists and investors believe that increased consumer spending—which translates to a lower savings rate—is positive advice? Where is the common sense behind this belief?

When I was a student in the economics department of Sydney University in Australia, our professor warned us against the economic theories in textbooks written by supposedly highly recognized academic theoreticians. He said that many economists go up into "ivory towers" and start spinning out theories embellished with highly technical language but completely useless for application in the real world. When we take up the ideas of vision and fortune in the next chapter, we shall be able to better comprehend the above comments. As we come to the end of the book, we will look at economic theory applications that are consistent with everyday common sense and wisdom.

An appreciation of sound economic theory does not mean blind adherence to its more simple generalizations. A theory certainly helps us understand solutions to problems in the real world. However, most theories that work under certain real-world circumstances may not be applicable under other circumstances. A theory narrows its field of focus when seeking to provide solutions for a problem such as high unemployment. The theory includes generalizations that do not solve the problem as it exists in certain economic, political, and social situations, and may even aggravate it. However, this does not mean that the theory is useless. Under some circumstances the theory may work perfectly. If I were to clarify what I mean in the language of economics, it may mean a defense of Keynesian theory and its present-day validity. In later chapters, this book will elaborate why the author is advocating the use of Keynesian tools of government. These tools will help to alleviate the high unemployment figures and low investment rates presently prevailing. Keynesian theory suggests that increased government spending when unemployment is high and economic activity is low will mean an increase in aggregate level of spending and job creation.

In the social sciences of politics and economics, policy formulators and decision makers must look at as broad a picture as possible. They can then see which theory best suits the given situation and which measures can be used effectively to solve the problems. The practice of theory requires a broad, deep a vision suitable for complex and varying circumstances. Theory, by definition, simplifies by using concepts that are comprehensible in its application to the real world. If a theory is not simplified and comprehensible, it should not be used. An example is the trust of institutional securities buyers of the ratings based on complex mathematical models that were incomprehensible to decision makers.

Another example is derivatives. These were sold as complex financial securities, but their value, risk, and liquidity were known only to the highly sophisticated, savvy investor. If seen in the right perspective, it is very simple to perceive their true value, risk, and liquidity. To simplify, derivatives can be used either as a hedge to mitigate risks or as pure speculation. American International Insurance Group (AIG) was really a "sucker," as one professor of economics put it, and many others arrived at the same conclusion. To speculate with such a large amount of capital is foolhardy, whether for an insurance-industry institution or for a small business. The insurance industry is so highly critical to the financial security of a people that it must, of necessity, be conservative in its investment decisions. Speculative activities by institutions have to be either tightly regulated or disallowed.

The unemployed are asking when the jobs will return. Many more of the unemployed ask when the economy will recover. Many of the employed also ask if there may be more layoffs. More are even afraid that their jobs will be outsourced or even eliminated.

Globalization has obviously impacted millions of average Americans negatively. It is true that globalization has made imported household products much more affordable than they would be if produced domestically. However, jobs and opportunities for millions of working-class Americans went offshore and are now more scarce here. This has caused a dilemma since people are now asking where their jobs will come from—jobs that pay as well as they used to. But protectionism, although considered by many thoughtful economists, is not truly a productive option.

Some major strategic plans have been conceived and have been set in place by the government, among them renewable energy, more efficient infrastructure programs, and a more vigorous marketing of America as a foreign tourism destination. These programs are positive approaches for job creation. They will also reduce the foreign trade deficit and raise efficiency levels and thereby provide a more competitive capability for American enterprises. Protectionism, on the other hand, would result in consumer goods inflation, which would reduce the real incomes of average Americans.

Thoughtful working-class Americans are also asking what they can do to help alleviate their present insecure financial circumstances.

New technology seems to be the only other card that America could hope to play to generate jobs. The question, though, is whether new technologies can provide enough jobs to replace those that have been outsourced. And do the newly unemployed have the aptitude to learn the new skills required for the new technologies? Some cynics may even say that new job opportunities may also be outsourced to other countries.

It is mainly the savings and capital of wage-earning Americans—pensions, insurance policies, bank deposits, and retained corporate earnings—that finance American business. This is why, in spite of a relatively small number of mega-rich people, American capitalism is called "people's capitalism." Yet, business seems to be outsourcing technical jobs, including research positions as well as factory and office jobs. This, along with excessive consumer spending, has resulted in a huge foreign debt. We are now the largest foreign debtor in the world. Only three and a half decades ago, we were the world's largest creditor nation. Our present circumstances have reduced substantially the capability of our domestic capital base to finance growth opportunities. This is the reality.

Whatever economic growth we hope for will have to be financed by foreign borrowings. The printing of more of our currency, in the hope of financing growth, is futile. It will just cause inflation, either of asset prices or consumer goods prices, due to the depreciation of the dollar vis-à-vis foreign currencies. Feeding more printed money to the economy may just raise consumer spending levels, thereby keeping the savings rate inadequate for investment needs. As I mentioned, this is an inflationary move; even if the nominal wealth of America increases greatly, its real wealth is a lot less. Inflation in assets or consumer goods prices will just make us less competitive and aggravate our present tough circumstances.

Now, do these present circumstances, and the chance that we may fail at this point to reverse the negative direction of the economy, mean that foreigners will have a greater share in the national income of our population? Yes. Foreigners will have the greater economic security and higher incomes which many of us will lose.

How much erosion of economic and political power will result from a failure to alter or reverse our present circumstances and direction? Is the present direction alterable? Can the present group of political, economic, and social leaders muster the spirit and the intellectual focus to work together to alter our present circumstances and change the direction of American political and economic power?

There are the health care and SSI issues. Those presently on Medicare seem intransigent towards any changes to their benefits and its resulting financial security. Are they in touch with the economic reality of our circumstances? The health care bill, just approved by President Obama, provides social justice. But is it financially feasible, given our economic reality? At present, we do not know if it will mean lower medical insurance costs for businesses. The government insists, however, that it will reduce medical insurance costs for business, the individual, and government. This will result from the spreading of insurance risks and costs over a much greater number of people. In many sectors of the economy, it is the high total cost of worker benefits that has rendered our economy much less competitive vis-à-vis the rest of the world, especially emerging markets. Our higher productivity as workers is not sufficient to make up for the high costs of wage benefits.

Will the new health care bill also reduce the rising health care costs to the government, the burden of which is estimated to be unfundable in the not-too-distant future? Will it mean much greater budget deficits in the short term if the unemployed and underemployed cannot find employment? It is the belief of this author that the present huge budget deficit, low personal savings rate, and economic conditions will lead to inflation that will further erode real incomes and thus our standard of living.

The Federal Reserve Board (the "Fed") may realize that their hopes to stimulate demand with their loose monetary policy will result in inflation. It will come in higher price earnings ratios of shares in the stock exchanges or housing and commercial property, if not in consumer goods and services prices. To some of the more astute in the fixed-income securities markets, the present very low interest rates on bonds (and their resulting higher value) are untenable and therefore high risk. Insurance companies and pension funds, which buy thirty-year bonds at current interest rates, will in all probability, suffer substantial losses in the future.

Inflation will erode competitiveness of our domestic factors of production and reduce "real" incomes. The depreciation of our currency will mean improved competitiveness for our export industries. But it will also mean a higher cost on imports, which is mainly for consumer goods. This will mean inflation, though this course of action is a palliative rather than a cure for our presently unfavorable economic circumstances. Depreciation is not a truly positive course of action.

Obesity, a large number of government subsidy-dependent single-parent households, disturbing education trends, drug use and addiction, and rising violence among the young, both in and out of school, are among the most pressing social issues today. One of our major economic issues is the shortfall in supply of adequate numbers of engineers and scientists and other professionals. The education trend is going to worsen the economy on these needs. But given other factors, are there really sustainable lifetime opportunities for those professions, as compared to, say, physical therapist jobs?

A relevant question, too, is whether the present educational system can prepare a well-educated student body for college. The second question is whether that is suitable for the whole student population. Not all students may have the aptitude or other economic wherewithal for college. Many students may have to help out in the financial necessities of their family. Many students may just not be interested in theory which is major part of college. Also, it is not possible in the foreseeable future to have a strong dynamic economy without factories and industries.

The aspirations of the youth vary to a great extent. The student entering high school, and even those in the later stages of elementary school, can be made aware, and informed of the various skills, knowledge, and aptitudes that are required of all the different occupations. We know that they should know trends and needs in the workplace. This is so that they will be informed as to which types of jobs are diminishing in numbers and those which are increasingly available. They need to know the importance of growing and learning as a person throughout life. This is even more necessary in this age of globalization.

Can the common and almost universal needs of the workplace, such as typing at a required minimum speed, be taught, even at an early age? Can students, who are not and cannot be motivated to study a broad range of subjects by the current crop of teachers, be trained, even in high school, to become chefs, waiters, warehouse managers, etc.? These questions are based on my perception that children are more aware of social issues due to their own family life and their contact with friends, plus television and computer content. There are, in other words, at present, very different and varied aspirations and motivations among the youth, than from the learning opportunities being given them. The educational means and standards do not seem to correspond to the aspirations, motivations, and social awareness of the young.

The economic and social dynamics of the times, and the speed of change, make it even more imperative to reexamine the educational system. We need to perceive what has to be done to educate the young on the basis of the reality of what they can achieve, given their motivational level, intellect and aptitudes. Moral, intellectual, and emotional education is critical for the young. I often wonder if television programming and the vogue for computer games can be harnessed to help the young achieve a desirable educational end. Schooling alone may not achieve that objective.

Is educational reform necessary? The answer would seem to rest with the abilities of the education leaders to perceive what we can hope to achieve with the students and teachers of today.

In later chapters, we will cover the various options that are available to enterprise, workers, and government to reverse the erosion of American political, economic, and social power.

I believe that the era of American unilateralism or hegemony in the international political and economic arena, is over. I also think that, regardless of our trade differences, we need to make China an ally. Much of the government policy of China is no longer based on centralized planning, nor is it really a command economy anymore. It is no longer truly based on the communist ideal of preference for the common worker. Because the entrepreneurial and managerial class has been given so much freedom in the decision-making process, China's elite is no longer suppressed. Resource allocation, and even enterprise income distribution policy, has been left almost entirely to the entrepreneurial and managerial elite.

America's main concerns are national security, foreign affairs and trade, the dollar's stability and/or purchasing power, full employment and growth, social security, and health care. Responsibility for full employment and the stability of the value of the dollar have been delegated to the Fed. However, today, the burden of alleviating high unemployment levels is undertaken mostly through fiscal-policy measures. The government has enacted legislation to substantially increase infrastructure needs, including renewable energy and improved energy efficiency. It also now gives tax credits to small business and to all businesses for additions to the work force.

The major social and business needs for health-care reform seem to conflict with one another. Health care costs have to be both reduced in dollar amounts and brought into line with an annual rate of inflation, that is, in line with the rate of inflation of the Consumer Price Index (CPI). Historical rates of inflation for health care have been way above the CPI rate. Secondly, a huge number of baby boomers—those born shortly after World War II—will be retiring and going on Medicare and SSI pensions. This will add substantially to the deficit. At the same time, it will also mean higher health care costs as the retirees progress into old age. Thirdly, government announcement of the number of those without health insurance seems to be understated. For the sake of social and political justice, as well as the need of enterprise for a healthy workforce, there is a consensus that all people must be covered by medical insurance. Insuring all people will even increase the proportionate share of health care in the Gross Domestic Product (GDP).

The task is formidable. The resolution of the health care issue is crucial to America. Government cannot, at present, afford to finance both Medicare and Medicaid, given the numbers of the baby boomers that will be retiring within the next five to ten years. American enterprise and its workers need a major change from the unrelenting rate of very high inflation rates of health care. Otherwise, the result will be a loss of competitiveness among American enterprises. Health care costs will be one of the major contributors to the decline of America to the level of a third-world economy unless this and other issues are resolved. America may end up like Russia, without much economic muscle and without a significant a role in world affairs. Russia has its military muscle but it no longer has much influence outside its traditional borders.

Security, both from within and without, is the foremost concern of government. The main concern is how long America can afford to maintain its current defense postures and how soon we can extricate ourselves from the war in Afghanistan.

The economic power erosion is real and progressive; in the middle of April, 2010, interest rates were raised a little. This did not cause alarm in the financial market, but the increase in rates did mean asset inflation. Housing prices are still falling in some parts of the country and rising fractionally in others. The additional total costs over five years for a mortgage means higher acquisition and rental prices. The Fed may have to raise interest rates due to inflation which would be caused by the depreciation of the dollar.

America has been pressing the Chinese government to revalue their currency, the Yuan. This would mean a depreciation or devaluation of the US dollar relative to the Yuan and will bring inflation and higher interest rates. It could bring asset inflation in real estate and a higher cost of capital to enterprise.

Even if China does not revalue its currency to balance its trade, our government may eventually have to impose a tariff on our imports of export products from China. The size and rate of growth of our trade deficit is already untenable. Our unemployment levels, and the overall US dollar holdings of China, erode our economic power. Our trade deficit is a problem that must be resolved.

To make matters worse, the budget deficit will substantially exceed annual savings of the American people. This, in turn, means substantial increases in the foreign debt and added inflationary pressures.

China, Brazil, India, and Russia, at present, do not present a competitive capability in technology innovation or in other capital-intensive industries. The present financial condition and direction of America was the product of the Cold War and loose monetary policies for more than 20 years before Fed chairman Bernanke. The false belief was that greed was good (rather than dangerous, with its tendency to cloud vision, perspective, and balance). The long, prevailing belief declared that very high levels of personal consumption equaled full employment. The rising foreign debt was presented also as not a major threat or challenge. Many corporate leaders too, responded too hastily to offshore outsourcing, or failed at all to act sooner to rising loss of competiveness, for example, in the automotive industry.

So far, all these suggest that America's future is uncertain, threatening to many and, to say the least, very challenging.

The destiny of America, of course, lies in the determination of the political, economic, and social leaders—and our citizens—to respond with the courage, intellectual focus, and spirit needed to turn the economy around.

There is still time to reverse the direction our economy is heading in. The bright side in our present situation is that the policies and measures needed to alter the present direction are all in our hands.

The odds are in our favor, and we will be able to resolve our present problems. America will remain first among equals in the world. But for most Americans, a certain amount of real income will have to decline.

We hope the health care legislation just enacted will solve the problem of a large segment of our population being uninsured medically. Additional high unemployment levels, unless corrected, will mean a continuing decline of America's political and economic power.

The trade friction with China over its currency valuation policies will have to be resolved. Free trade needs to have correspondingly free markets for currency rates, and for unsubsidized goods and services traded. Otherwise, unsustainable trade between countries will continue.

America can no longer afford to continue having huge trade deficits with so many countries. We have so much foreign debt we virtually have to borrow from other countries just to finance investments spending by enterprise and government. This leads to a weakening of our political and economic power and influence vis-à-vis the rest of the world.

Can these weaknesses be reversed? If yes, then over what period of time? When will the erosion in "real" incomes stop? When will it reverse course towards growth of incomes again? When will most of us know economic security in our jobs and careers?

For later chapters, we will give our view of what measures will need to come about and the time frames required for a return to economic security.

(1) The Financial Crisis of 2007 en. Wikipedia.org/wiki/financial_crisis_2007

(2) Bureau of Economic Analysis/National Income Accounts/Current Personal Savings Rate bea.gov/newsreleases/national

(3) U.S.A.- Government Budget 2010 - 2011

CHAPTER 2

VISION AND FORTUNE

Wise men tell us that we live in darkness and seek wisdom, which provides light. Wisdom gives us vision in our daily lives, as well as in our field of endeavor. Sound vision would enable us to live and work more effectively and efficiently with others, as well as with economic and political resources. In the fields of religion, the sciences, and the arts, we primarily seek wisdom, knowledge, and common sense.

Prevailing beliefs can be for better or worse, depending upon the soundness of the vision and the rationale behind our beliefs. In the pursuit of knowledge in the sciences or the arts, our observations and experiences lead us to establish theories and principles. The latter helps us apply them in practice, for the purpose of improving our way of life. Thus, we learn that laws and principles help establish order and progress by the "light" they give.

However, men who are recognized for wisdom tell us that much of what we believe is illusion, fad, or a belief in principles that are inconsistent with reality. They tell us that reality is not easily perceived, for it requires a sound, realistic knowledge of human nature. The spiritually undeveloped (or underdeveloped) person suffers from a lack of perception of what a "good life" or what a person of "real substance" really is. This "darkness" or ignorance among people, including leaders, is the product of sin, which is derived from a Greek word meaning error. Sins of ambition, greed, pride, and lust lead men to repeated warfare, economic recessions and depressions, bankruptcies, and other adversities. The need for able leadership and the spiritually sound choices of people to lead in the political, economic, and social spheres cannot be understated. Continuously changing circumstances require sound vision and leadership.

The globalization of business activities presents both opportunities and risks that may bring adversity because of their complexity. The element of luck must also be taken into consideration. However, we do not know how, and whether, luck will favor one or the other. We do know from history that in conflict or competition, luck plays a role in outcomes. Luck is the product of unintended consequences or circumstances and is an important factor in the affairs of men and society.

Vision implies perceiving the full reality of one's circumstances and the various courses of action one can take. As an example, awareness of the present circumstances of the economy and its direction requires gathering data and news about them. The people affected must somehow measure the risks and consequences involved, if the present direction is not corrected. This is so, since we are aware of the present adverse circumstances of our economy. We also know of the various severe problems that are beginning to surface.

The probability of success in reversing unfavorable circumstances and direction requires judgment, and judgment requires vision derived from wisdom, knowledge, and common sense. Judgment is arrived at with measured risks using probabilities, for example, fluctuations in the rate of unemployment.

How does one know if he or she has the wisdom, knowledge, and common sense to arrive at sound conclusions? How can anyone know the accuracy of the measures sought and of the probabilities involved? Is it possible, in the first place, to arrive at any sound measures of risks in this arena?

The answer to all these questions depends on the individual or the group, and the amount of wisdom, knowledge, and common sense it will take to accurately assess the various probable outcomes.

To illustrate: a businessman or individual seeking to get a loan will have to evaluate under what circumstances he or she can repay the loan. He will also have to consider under what circumstances he might be unable to repay the loan, and what circumstances might produce that outcome. After that, he will have to assess whether the outcome will mean bankruptcy or whether he will have to sell some assets in order to repay the loan.

Most people who borrow prepare a budget reflecting incomes and cash flows from the use of the loan. Many businessmen and accountants use simple balance sheet ratios such as debt-service to tell them if leveraging their financial operations is within safety standards. If the debt-service cover is high enough to make it safe to borrow a certain amount, they usually make the decision to borrow.

However, a budget must be realistic. Mathematical models must be prepared with adequate judgment, which means using wisdom garnered from past experience, knowledge of business, and common sense. If greed or lack of prudence—and therefore lack of care in the preparation of the models—prevails, the mathematical models will be totally unrealistic.

This was, in the author's opinion, the cause of the real-estate bubble and the resulting financial crisis of 2009. I also believe that the preparers of the model were not adequately advised of the change in the underlying circumstances under which the historical data reflected loss and repayment ratios or experiences. Applicants for loans lied about their financial circumstances while unbelievably lax credit standards unprecedented in American credit history prevailed.

The buyers of the securities which failed, should not have just relied on the ratings of the credit-rating agencies, but should, at least, have asked the relevant questions. This requires prudence. The financing of real estate mortgages was accomplished mainly by selling collateralized debt obligations. These complex financial instruments were sold to pension funds, insurance companies, and to banks worldwide. They were what was rated by Moody's, Fitch, and S&P. This process made it possible to finance almost limitless amounts of real estate mortgages. The fundamentals of credit and collection management require four criteria for measuring the risk of loss. They are a) the character of the borrower, b) adequate collateral, c) the capacity to repay, and d) business, industry, and economic conditions. As most people realize now the ratings were faulty. Credit and collection principles were not fully applied to credit risk evaluation.

A couple of listed public companies, engaged in the manufacture of motor vehicle parts, went bankrupt in 2009. Like several other companies in similar circumstances, the failure was not so much because of the lack of available credit, but because of the substantial deterioration in their sales as original equipment maker to the motor vehicle industry, especially the "Big Three" American manufacturers. The Big Three, with the exception of the Ford Motor Corporation, went bankrupt. It was not just the competition that reduced them to this state, but consumers' sharp cutback in spending in 2008. Consumers, as most analysts knew, were spending far above their means. Common sense (which is not really common) should have led decision makers to realize that a day of reckoning must arrive.

Consumers, as the finance companies and banks knew, had been taking out home equity loans made possible by ever-rising home prices. When home prices started deteriorating at the end of 2006, it should have warned the business community that the day of reckoning was near. Prudence, or at least more care was needed in the formulation of risk policy, specifically leveraging policy.

Let us turn to the subject of religion. A religion teaches a set of spiritual laws whose interpretation and practice vary from one religion to another as well as from one person to another.

Spiritual laws essentially seek to teach us how to relate to a Higher Being, to others, and toward ourselves and our circumstances. It teaches love of God and obedience to the spiritual laws, which comes from him and promises to lead us to a fuller, richer life.

The great religions, in one way or another, teach that the practice of their religion will lead to inner peace as well as to abundance, which results in a richer, fuller life. Religious admonitions to have faith, to love, to forgive, and to give, are designed to teach us what to do. Mostly, it does not completely teach us why the obedience to the laws will lead us to fuller, richer life and success in our endeavors.

Religion teaches that the laws will lead to harmony, persistence, joy, prudence, and patience.

It is common knowledge that every condition, process, and consequence in any field is governed by laws. The spiritual laws—to have faith, to love, to give, and to forgive—produce positive results. They provide the highest probabilities for success, harmony and inner peace, as well as peace with others. The spiritual laws also teach humility, patience, and forbearance and avoidance of bias and prejudice. The full interpretation of these laws requires a measure of reflection and meditation. We must seek to know the truth or the reality of the kind of person we are, stripped of illusions and fantasies. We do this through reflection and meditation on the laws and on our lives.

We reflect, measure, and judge our actions and motivations according to these laws. An honest appraisal will teach us our shortcomings as well as our strengths. Essentially, we will get to know the worst and the best of ourselves. Our chances of living a fuller, richer life will depend on our honest self-appraisal and our willingness and strength to abide by these laws.

What a fuller, richer life means varies from person to person. Through our self-examination, we learn the causes of our failures, as well as the basis of our successes. Through our reflections on our lives, we perceive the reality of our human condition. We realize whether we have been grounded or whether we are "up in the air." We also realize whether we were thoughtful and generous in our interpersonal relations, or thoughtless and selfish.

Then, through our reflections, we realize that we have essentially been living in darkness, that is, unaware of ourselves and our actions. We begin to know when we have been self-defeating or sufficiently enlightened about our goals and our means of achieving them. Finally, we come to realize the common human condition. We realize why greed, pride, ambition, lust, sloth, envy, bigotry, and other sins (or errors) cause failures and suffering among men, women, and children. We fully realize why a lack of harmony and the existence of enmity between men and in society generally are due to the underdeveloped spirit that is manifested as the human condition.

We perceive the varying degrees of darkness in men and society, as well as the degree of enlightenment. Some men or societies seem to live mostly in darkness, while others have extraordinary wisdom and common sense.

We perceive why it is extremely difficult, intellectually, to discover truth in the arts or sciences without an investment of faith and humility. We realize that the darkness caused by sin or error covers or colors the judgment of men and societies, and brings about the greatest probability of failure. We will then fully understand why Jesus Christ, the prophet, said when dying upon the cross, "Father, forgive them for they know not what they do." (Luke 23:34) One can finally perceive why and how he was right for loving people in spite of the sufferings they inflicted upon him. He fully knew that the enlightened person, as opposed to the ignorant, is a beautiful human being, worthy of the great love that he possessed. We also understand why God loves us in spite of our shortcomings.

We also perceive that spiritual development is one of the many challenges God bestows upon a person. He fully realizes that deep within a person is a love of challenge and a struggle to lift up the human spirit, leading to a truly full and rich life. He has instilled in the spirit of men and women a love of challenge and adventure. These are the main reasons why wise men and women say "enjoy the journey far more than the arrival at your goals and ambitions."

With reflection, one discovers the causes of his or her failures, perceives the human condition, and, if truly enlightened, develops compassion rather than hate towards oneself and others. One learns the truth that hate or a lack of love and compassion toward others is not self-love, but also a manifestation of a lack of love and compassion toward oneself. This is especially evident in a time of personal failure.

In times of failure, men often turn against themselves. Some commit suicide, some take to alcohol or drugs or loose sex and other self-destructive behaviors. This is why the spiritual laws teach love and compassion. This potential for spiritual development speaks the truth about men and women, that they are made in the image of God. This is why God loves us, and why we say that all men are brothers, and why there is one God. This is why all men and women are beautiful and lovable in spite of their shortcomings. This is the author's vision encompassing his beliefs. We each have our own vision and beliefs.

When one overcomes sin or error, it is like clearing one's vision of whatever blocks the vision and getting a true and exhilarating view of reality based on truth. The truth, in my opinion, is that we are all given by the Creator the challenges to overcome the darkness and the capacity to be co-creators for a more beautiful world. One realizes, even during one's darkest hours, that life is meant to be more beautiful, and that we should be more hopeful and believe that we will prevail.

Hopefully, these reflections will ease the discomfort felt by many, given our present, very trying economic circumstances. Hopefully also, those who seek to profit from the tragic circumstances facing many of our people will reflect on the morality underlying their actions. If the actions of those who, for example, speculate in the real-estate markets at the present time are within the confines of a measure of generosity and fairness to all, then we will recover sooner from the recession. Otherwise, we will just bring in more regulations, rather than the needed moral restraint upon our markets.

Regulation is welcomed in many circumstances. It is just that it is difficult to formulate sound regulation and enforce it. Regulation also increases the cost of doing business, for it means spending for regulators. Where moral restraint is extremely difficult to observe, regulations and regulators are a necessity so that people may have a more just society. Note that while regulation entails costs, such costs may prove beneficial in the long term.

It is also important to realize that with the Creator's love, comes the promise of challenge for us and redemption from the darkness. Redemption from sin or error, rather than hellfire and brimstone, in my opinion, is the purpose behind the teachings of the great religions. Although I have read some books on Islam, the Bhagavad Gita, and Buddhism, I know the Christian faith much more intimately, so I will quote again from the Bible. In the New Testament Jesus says, "I have not come to judge the world, but to save it." (John 12:47) With him and his teachings comes redemption from the darkness through its observance or adherence. That is what he taught.

This knowledge of the human condition may give you some perception as to why some men or women are possessed of an indomitable spirit, while others break or commit suicide and engage in self-destructive behaviors in times of struggles and failures.

You may now realize how the biographies of different men and women, their failures and successes, and their ultimate fate, reveal the validity of the spiritual laws.

The degree of one's enlightenment governs the true reality of one's perception of other laws that govern in the sciences and the arts. Any inconsistency or conflict between a theory in the arts and sciences, and the spiritual laws, usually implies a false theory. It usually implies that the observations of conditions or behavior from the theory were inaccurate.

The degree of enlightenment is the basic frame of reference by which one perceives the true reality from other laws in politics, economics, business, and other fields in the arts and sciences.

To illustrate, the present rate of change in technology, demography, globalization, new nutrition ideas and health care standards, and other changes, such as political decisions affecting people and the economy, make medium and long-term economic forecasting virtually impossible.

The probabilities of financial risks facing the worker, the investor, enterprise, and the economy generally, arrived at using historical data, are terribly inadequate.

In reality, the future direction or growth (or reduction) in earning power and even the chances of survival of particular enterprises, are highly unpredictable. In statistical terms, enterprise is too subject to random events, and therefore, its stock market share price movements, would be a "random walk" for the short term. Random walk means that price or cost movement of a material or stock market share price will be unpredictable using historical data.

The realization of our limitations is the reason why spiritual teachings like humility and prudence are required for successful living.

One's reflections and meditations on spiritual teachings and their application in life, helps one realize that they teach the art of fine living. They ensure one a greater number of possibilities in life, with greater probability of success. If we observe closely, we find that greed, pride, and other basic errors or sins have led men and women to downfall and ruin, even death, with negative impact on others as well.

Christianity teaches us not to judge others. Men and women emphasize different values in differing degrees. Wise men and women know that giving up some things could bring more of other things in life—materially, spiritually, intellectually, and emotionally. Many know that in some cases "less is more," foregoing one thing for another personally preferred thing or values like time, family, or another good or service. Every man or woman will have to decide for themselves what a rich and full life means and the happiness and fulfillment it brings.

In the soul of every man and woman is the gift of God of particular things of value to them. These they must seek over time as the soul seeks to manifest itself in one's heart, mind, and emotions. The destiny of every man or woman is governed by how much they listen to their soul, seeking to manifest itself through the spirit and the heart. So listen to your heart if it seeks the good of oneself and others. It is often better and wiser to listen to the heart rather than the mind or the emotions.

That men and women are made in the image of God reinforces the truth that deep within, all are beautiful. Love is appreciating what is beautiful about oneself and others, and overlooking the external aspects of a person such as looks, money, or status. Overlooking minor faults and seeking to overcome them in oneself are part of spiritual teachings. It is from this perspective that the author seeks to evaluate the strengths of the American people without meaning to overlook any major weakness in the formulation of assumptions and conclusions as to the various possible future conditions that could evolve in the economy. Many conclusions are basically within the author's own personal evaluation of the spirit and the will, heart, and intellect of the American people.

In this book, the subject of risk will cover the economy, business, and the worker sectors. Risk is measured so that the government, the leaders of business and non-profit organizations, the investor, the wage earner, and the consumer can make decisions that counter or take advantage of either adverse or favorable conditions. Risk measurement is the process wherein the statistical method in decision making is used. It uses historical, statistical data as well as subjective assignment of probabilities or certain conditions or happenings at a projected future time. The final probabilities of various degrees of loss indicate whether the risk of loss of, for example, a leveraged final position of an enterprise, is high or medium or low. It could assign a probability of 60 percent out of 100 percent of a loss of so much or even bankruptcy or insolvency, which means high risk. The decision maker of the enterprise may find 10 percent risk of insolvency acceptable with a given financial leverage. Another decision maker may decide that even a one percent chance of insolvency is not worth taking, so he would prefer an unleveraged financial structure policy. The responses of decision makers also depend on whether the returns from a course of action taken, are sufficient or inadequate relative to its risks.

To illustrate: the investor would want to know the profit or loss probabilities in the value of a security and its probable returns. To the "bears" in the securities markets, the potential losses of the value of a security offers profit opportunities. On the other hand, such losses would imply unfavorable circumstances for the "bulls." The standard for risks and returns often implies that taking high risks implies high returns. Low risks generally offer low returns. Such, however, is not always the case. Some high risks, in reality, may offer only very little return, or even losses. Reality is not always consonant with the common or prevailing view. Warren Buffett, one of the world's richest investors, has made his fortune by taking a course of action contrary to the prevailing view. Peter Lynch, a well-known asset manager, made investment decisions along different paths from the prevailing market behavior. These two examples perceived a reality far different from that of the crowd. Both men exhibited vision, prudence, and self-control of emotions and impulses uncommon to the crowd. Such are the possibilities from well-developed spiritual qualities emanating from the virtues of prudence and self-control.

CHAPTER 3

THE HOUSING SECTOR

Housing, one of our most basic needs, commands approximately 34.1 percent [4] of median income earnings. In America, this principally consists of mortgage interest, utilities expenses, and property taxes. The lower-income groups spend a greater proportion of their disposable income for housing. Added to this expense are principal amortizations, which would bring up the total proportion of housing costs to disposable incomes. (These figures were derived from the latest Consumer Expenditure Survey conducted by the U.S. Department of Labor since 2007.) The higher-income groups may or may not necessarily spend a smaller percentage of their personal disposable income on housing. Many in this group have more than one house.

Since the end of 2007 to 2010, housing prices have dropped substantially. However, most Americans' earned incomes have dropped even more substantially. As we all know, delinquencies and foreclosures, which began occurring in earnest at the end of 2006, are still high, even as of the end of March 2010.

The charts below show that the speculative fever which led to the housing bubble and the resulting fall in housing prices, has not completely disappeared. Price fluctuations show substantial rises and falls in median home prices within a period of only one year.

Subject	Occupied housing units	Margin of Error	Owner-occupied housing units	Margin of Error	Renter-occupied housing units	Margin of Error
Coal or coke	0.1%	+/-0.1	0.1%	+/-0.1	0.1%	+/-0.1
All other fuels	2.3%	+/-0.1	2.8%	+/-0.1	1.4%	+/-0.1
No fuel used	0.9%	+/-0.1	0.5%	+/-0.1	1.6%	+/-0.1
PERCENT IMPUTED						
Units in structure	1.5%	(X)	(X)	(X)	(X)	(X)
Year structure built	17.6%	(X)	(X)	(X)	(X)	(X)
Rooms	6.6%	(X)	(X)	(X)	(X)	(X)
Bedrooms	2.8%	(X)	(X)	(X)	(X)	(X)
Plumbing facilities	1.8%	(X)	(X)	(X)	(X)	(X)
Kitchen facilities	2.4%	(X)	(X)	(X)	(X)	(X)
Vehicles available	0.8%	(X)	(X)	(X)	(X)	(X)
Telephone service available	0.9%	(X)	(X)	(X)	(X)	(X)
House heating fuel	2.2%	(X)	(X)	(X)	(X)	(X)

Source: U.S. Census Bureau, 2006-2008 American Community Survey

[5] Data Source National Association of Realtors

Monthly Fluctuations in Median Home Prices by Region

In Las Vegas, where the author resides, the degree of speculation was among the heaviest in the country. "Paper" and real fortunes were made virtually without the use of personal capital or risk money. Those who had exited from all their housing acquisitions early in 2006 would have made a killing, and I met a few who did. However, as far as I know, most of the heavy speculators lost all their paper profits, as did so many others in the country. I realized as early as mid-2003 that the expectations of most people were unrealistic.

In San Francisco's outlying communities, thirty-year-old 2-3 small bedroom houses were selling for as high as $1 million. By the third quarter of 2003, a community leader in the Bay Area stated publicly that current reasonable housing prices were affordable to only 15 percent of the population living in San Francisco and the Bay Area. This statement implied that the rest of the working population lived in crowded and relatively unpleasant housing conditions. At that time, with the appearance of the ARMS (Adjustable Rate Mortgages) and the no-down-payment phenomenon, it was clear to many that there was mindlessness and lack of common sense prevailing among large numbers of the population. The money flowing into the real estate markets was being called "funny money." Only a few were listening to any of those sounding the alarm as early as 2003.

In the third quarter of 2005, a real estate agent I knew had accumulated $3 million from nothing but "flipping" properties, even without remodeling, and holding on to houses for as little as three months. I encouraged her at that time to cash in her winnings and place them in fixed income securities and to look at realistic income levels of the working and retired population living in Las Vegas, most of who at that time were earning only slightly above the minimum wage. It was only the continuous high living of the American working population coming to Las Vegas that enabled waiters, casino dealers, hotel housekeepers, and taxi drivers to earn even more than the median income earner through tips or gratuities.

The high living of the American working population was made possible by loose credit conditions prevailing at that time. Las Vegas, being essentially a tourist destination emphasizing gaming, drinking, and other expensive pleasures, naturally brought in a good amount of cash in the form of tips. In Las Vegas, real estate and mortgage brokering should be mindful that the majority of the wage-earning group makes only $9-$11 gross per hour. The exceptions, of course, are the professionals and businessmen and businesswomen.

As of July 1, 2008, there were an estimated 129,065,264 housing units available in the United States. [6] This was a substantial increase from 116,295,266 on July 1, 2000. [6] However, at the end of 2008, there were only 112,386,298 occupied housing units. [7] Renter-occupied housing units totaled 37,023,213. [7] Owner-occupied housing units totaled the balance of 75,363,085. [7] Today, at the end of the first quarter of 2010, it is most likely that the proportion of renters will have risen, relative to total owner-occupied housing. This is likely, given the present employment situation. Also, it is certain that the numbers of homeless people in the United States will have risen significantly.

The following chart illustrates the substantial rise in the rate of increase in housing prices starting in 1997. It also shows a substantial fall in housing prices from late 2006 to 2008. [8] It fell even further in 2009.

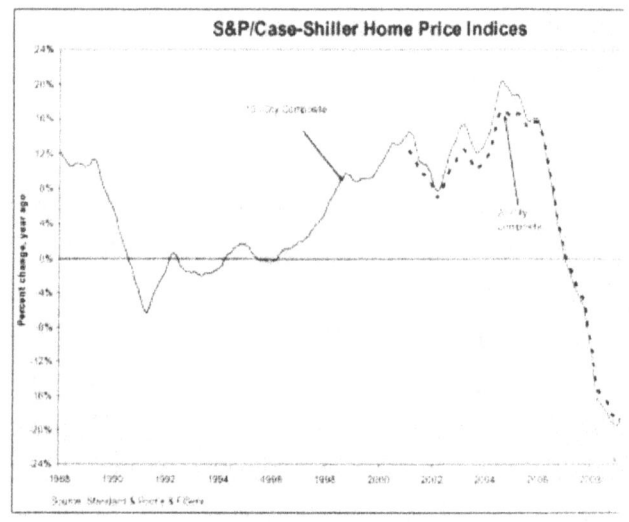

CASE-SCHILLER
HOME PRICE INDICES

It would therefore be advisable at this time that people who wish to purchase a house reflect a great deal before doing so. A drain of nearly 40 percent of household income means that a person should fully consider the difference between renting and home ownership, the location of the property, and other details. Banks and other mortgage lenders would do well also to have more detailed criteria for lending, given the various local socioeconomic conditions obtaining.

It would help if the potential buyer understood that living standards are not well understood by a large number of people. If he belongs to that very large (lower income) group, then he had better reconsider. Well considered living standards, based on the reality of one's circumstances, should govern the spending and saving allocations of one's income and assets. Excellent living standards, in turn, govern more essentially the quality and richness of life, rather than one's nominal standard of living. After all, the standard of living only means the total amount of money spent for living comfortably. One's living standards are governed by one's awareness of one's circumstances. Considering these will give one the values by which one may decide, among many other things, whether to seek more financial and economic security by saving a larger portion of income, or to live more modestly.

Common sense does not mean the common viewpoint or common perception. The common prevailing vision may not have been well or deeply considered before its adaptation. It may not therefore be consistent with a deeper and broader reality. Some truths like charity, hope, faith, and justice reveal universal and eternal realities related to the human condition and to people's potential. In other words, they enable you to judge whether your actions toward others are consistent with truths that are universal and eternal.

To give a concrete example: When the Medicare Bill was enacted into law, based on a vision of President Johnson's Great Society, it sought to provide medical and health care aid for the elderly population that no longer had the level of income to provide for themselves. The reality is that retirement income is not nearly enough to provide adequate medical care for the elderly.

The Social Security Act was passed in 1935 under the "New Deal" Administration of Franklin Delano Roosevelt as a social insurance program funded through payroll taxes. It was then conceived to provide economic and financial security to men and women who could no longer work for a living as productively. This program was founded on a vision that a society should be governed with an eye toward political, economic, and social justice.

These are the products of high aspirations of great men and women with a vision to build a great and lasting civilization. These aspirations and the vision they inspire are consistent with the spiritual truths of living by the laws of charity, hope, and faith, so that justice among men and women may prevail. If Rome, the Eternal City and seat of one of the greatest and longest-lived civilizations known to man, no longer prevails, it is because Christianity revealed truths which gave men their vision of justice consistent with truths that all men are brothers because they are equals before the Creator.

Given all these, let us now seek to perceive whether our own personal opinions on Medicare and Social Security policies are fair to ourselves and our fellow Americans. How do they apply to the housing sector? The lower income groups do not possess the education necessary for making sound investment decisions which would be required of privatized social insurance. The cost of housing would presently just be too high to afford if substantially higher provisions for privatized old age health care and pensions were required for the lower income groups.

Under present circumstances, and what can be seen for the foreseeable future, the American government will have neither the revenue nor the ability to reduce other spending to provide for this economic and social assistance to the elderly. Those who can provide medical and pension resources by their own means, must do so. Otherwise, the "real" standard of living—meaning having sufficient income and economic resources—will fall severely. The present level of medical care, health care, and pension income cannot be sustained by government alone.

Housing takes the biggest chunk of the incomes of wage earners. The cost of food, apparel, health care, and entertainment combined, is only about equal to total housing costs. Retirement provision, besides SSI, also requires substantial portions of one's income.

Savings placed in banks or other liquid financial instruments require substantial portions of one's income. Possession of liquid financial resources is absolutely necessary to provide a financial safety net in case of unfavorable events or emergencies.

To believe that high levels of consumer spending will stimulate the economy enough to provide for jobs is a self-defeating belief.

Most individuals must seek to provide for themselves to ensure an adequate standard of living and medical care. They must consider well and deeply how to live their lives so that their incomes and spending are consistent with their lifetime needs. To insist that government provide by any means, including a redistribution of wealth, is totally unrealistic.

Since housing is the biggest expense, the nation cannot afford speculation or general asset inflation. Speculation and asset inflation will destroy high living standards for at least 60 percent of the wage-earning population. Conspicuous consumption in the form of expensive housing for a significant number will bring cost-push inflation. The cost of materials, which are limited and getting scarcer, will be driven up. Lumber, copper wiring and other metals, cement, bricks, and imported housing components will rise, making comfortable housing less affordable to a very large swath of the population.

If housing everywhere in America rises continuously, housing will become unaffordable to retirees on fixed incomes, as well as median and lower-income earners. Given our present circumstances and resources and a time frame of twenty-five years, if present-day young wage earners do not live more frugally and provide for their old age, they will live a very economically deprived old age. Workers, as well as economic, political, and social leaders have to seek ways to avoid a very distressing future for the aged. Housing problems are also felt acutely by more than 30 percent of the population, including the employed. The housing bubble and the ensuing losses amounting to over $1 trillion will significantly lower the standard of living of at least the median and lower-income groups in America. This is because the losses of the banking sector and the resulting attempt of the

Fed to rescue them will ultimately bring about a loss in purchasing power of the currency.

For these reasons, it is the author's opinion that the call for regulation of the financial sector is imperative. It is unproductive and a waste of time pinning the blame on players in the political, economic, and financial scene. It is even more insane to ostracize the group that speculated like mad and caused the housing bubble.

As we stated earlier, speculation drove housing prices to unaffordable levels which, in the end, profited very few and impoverished the general population. It was not really the rise in interest rates caused by the Fed's policy to contain inflation that contributed to the collapse in housing prices. The prices of real estate and the volume of money invested in the sector were so high and heavy that it collapsed from its own weight.

To say that interest rates can be arbitrarily dictated at very low levels by simply printing more money is inconsistent with sound economic theory and principles. To oversimplify and overemphasize monetary theory will surely lead anyone and everyone astray. As my friends in college in Sydney, Australia, used to say, "that kind of belief propounded will lead us up the garden path." In other words, the promises are unrealistic.

Let's realize that the "darkness" which some wise men refer to as the common human condition, led to our present highly undesirable circumstances. Let's comfort ourselves that the conditions in other countries are even worse than ours.

Interest rates must be dictated by the investment needs of enterprise and government and the supply of funds from savings, enterprise, and government combined. If the demand and supply are not in balance, we will either cause inflation or trade deficits and the corresponding foreign debt to the extent of the trade deficit.

In later chapters we will explain the lack of validity of the prevailing view that moderate inflation is both good for job creation and economic growth. We will later seek to show that over the medium and long term, such a view will lead to an even larger underclass in our society.

Given the realities presented by the big economic picture, even the current housing prices are unaffordable for nearly 40 percent of wage earners. If the Fed's current interest rate policy is maintained for securing any other than short-term needs, sound economic recovery is not feasible. Purchasers of fixed income securities such as pension funds, insurance companies, and individuals, will lose substantially over the medium and long-term. When medium and long-term interest rates do rise, housing will become even more unaffordable. The economic and financial responsibilities and constraints on spending, for the individual, have become so much greater. I have sought to provide the underlying and other economic and social laws that resulted in these conclusions.

The more aware we are of our circumstances and the more enlightened we are, will determine our future economic circumstances.

To reiterate, living well is less a product of high income than of how much faith in ourselves we have. Hope, charity, and the optimism it gives us determine our level of dignity and respect. Here we respond to our responsibilities to ourselves and to others and the possession of adequate self-control to enable us to break free or at least live with dignity within our financial constraints. This will eventually impact on the dynamism and stability of our lives as well as the economy.

Living in more modest housing has become a necessity for more wage earners than it was a few decades ago. This is so, even despite technological advances and the substantial improvements it brought in productivity levels in the work place.

It is the author's sincerest hope to be perceived as "lighting a candle" that we may lead happier, fuller, and richer lives, and not to provide a bleak picture. It is to be hoped that we can all live truly better lives than the ones we are living now.

The common good, in the national interest, cannot be served by leaders alone. It requires the average man and woman to seek better conditions as participants in our political and economic life. As Confucius said many centuries ago, order and responsibility must be undertaken starting from the individual to the home, then the community, and then the nation. Our economic and social destiny as individuals and as a nation will be determined more by us than by our leaders alone. We certainly cannot afford an excessive preoccupation with personal interest. We must adequately consider realities and what is necessary for the common good.

We will surely end up as a third world country if we refuse to consider national and community interests in the pursuit of our personal interest. I lived long enough in a third world country to know what I am talking about. In some countries, people who practice a great deal of self-denial of material goods may be more engaged in self-centeredness than is consistent with the universal truth to practice charity. Many times in history, religious people were in great "darkness" themselves and led societies they influenced to ruin.

Every individual must seek the light and forge his or her own destiny as well as that of their nation, if they wish to live a fuller and richer life.

Big houses and fancy cars are not necessarily manifestations of a better quality of life. Life offers far more exciting and truly rewarding experiences than mansions, fancy cars, and beautiful women have to offer. Ask the peasant who is a joyful person if this isn't so. He will tell you that joy is something which wealth and rank by themselves cannot give. Ask the humble priest who has denied himself material goods and leisure to fully and soundly interpret his faith that he may practice and preach it faithfully. Ask him if this isn't so. Ask the average man and woman with a happy family life is this isn't so. Ask many others who sacrifice for others rather than remain self-preoccupied and self-indulgent. Ask the political leader who is trying to serve the interests of the country amid the heat and noise of the political battlefield. Ask the soldier in Afghanistan if life is more rewarding through self-indulgence and the pursuit of glamour and fame.

In spite of all this prevailing wisdom, very few live within their means and seek a more satisfying and rewarding life. We are solely responsible for our own final circumstances and destiny in life. This is more so today than in the last four or five decades, when business and government provided more economic security.

It is important to understand that we need to keep the cost of comfortable housing as low as possible for the needs of the low-wage workers. We need relatively low wages to make our economy more competitive in this age of globalization. The more competitive our economy is the more stable our employment situation. So many million jobs are dependent on our effectiveness in world export markets. If we become less competitive, due to higher wage and benefits costs to enterprise, we will lose our export markets. Then eventually we will lose our domestic markets.

If speculation or asset inflation occurs, we end up with a loss of markets and jobs. Affordable and comfortable housing is both a necessity for good living and demands a very large part of our disposable incomes. The more we spend on housing, the less we have for other vital purchases and for savings. This will affect both the vitality and productivity of the workforce, as well as other sectors of the economy where we have been forced to spend less.

The hope of making a fortune in real estate is really only realized under circumstances wherein high productivity and high wage enterprise locates its operations. Then the influx of very high income earners enables them to afford to bid up prime locations near the enterprise. Otherwise, increase in prices in real estate is nothing more than asset inflation. No one in real estate, in reality, gains from asset inflation. This is so for any kind of asset inflation, including those for share prices. People are imagining that they are getting wealthier in times of asset inflation, when in fact the currency is suffering from continuous loss of purchasing power.

When more stable asset prices prevail relative to value, higher employment productivity will improve our nominal and real incomes. If we save and invest, in reality we get wealthier or richer. With asset inflation, we are deluding ourselves as to our real incomes and wealth.

Sound sources of employment incomes are not possible if housing prices suffer from asset inflation. In this age of globalization, higher wage and the corresponding higher cost of living pressures will make our economy much less competitive. Jobs will be lost to imports and outsourcing will escalate.

(4)   Consumer Expenditures in 2007: U.S. Department of Labor, U.S. Bureau of Labor Statistics, April 2009, Report 1016

(5)   Real Estate ABC. Com http://www.Realestateabc.com. outlook/overall.htm

(6)   U.S. Census Bureau – American Factfinder – Annual Estimates of Housing Units for the United States and States April 1, 2000 – July 1, 2008

(7)   U.S. Census Bureau American Factfinder – Occupancy Characteristics

(8)   http://www.standardandpoors.com/sp/case/shiller/ home/price/indices/en/us

CHAPTER 4

THE FINANCIAL SECTOR

The financial crisis, with its losses in the trillions, was due to blind trust in the rating agencies, especially by people in the worldwide banking industry. The mathematical models used by Wall Street, as well as by the rating agencies, relied too heavily on historical performance and the consistently rising values of real estate beyond the cost of money. How blind these rating agencies were to reality. Investors were largely unaware.

As earlier mentioned, in 2003 a community leader in the Bay Area stated on TV that only 15 percent of households could afford adequate housing. Throughout America, housing prices had risen beyond affordability to the majority of the population. The response of the banking industry was to substantially lower lending standards. This encouraged a substantial increase in speculative activity. The rates of increase in housing prices became much higher.

The huge sums of money needed to finance large increases in demand for housing were made possible by what are known as collateralized debt obligations (CDOs) and structured investment vehicles (SIVs). There was a reckless change of rating risks in credit extension of individual housing mortgages from the lenders to the rating agencies in bundled form as CDOs. This was the fundamental flaw in credit extension.

As said earlier, mathematical modeling is highly subjective. To trust so much money on mathematical models produced by three rating agencies, as well as a few geniuses in the investment banking sector, was a bad move. This proves the truth that we live in darkness. Ignorance, greed, and pride brought about loss of assets and jobs and incomes in massive proportions.

Monetary policy is a financial tool used by the government to contain inflation. It is used as well to encourage enterprise and consumers to invest and spend more so as to stimulate the economy. Inflation fighting is when interest rates are raised so as to discourage both business and consumers from spending at present levels. During high rates of inflation, interest rates may even be raised several times.

This policy tool is achieved by increasing or decreasing the money supply in the economy through the purchase of treasury bills to increase the money supply when seeking to reduce interest rates on various financial fixed-income securities and interest-bearing bank deposits.

Selling treasuries, on the other hand, decreases the money supply in the economy and therefore discourages spending. A very large segment of the population knows that it is the Fed that is responsible for formulating this policy. The Fed also, in other ways, regulates the commercial and savings banks.

Other kinds of financial institutions, such as investment banks and others known generally as the "shadow" banking system are like money market funds. Money market funds commonly purchase treasuries and commercial papers (or CPs) for their portfolio.

As every investor knows, the money market funds take deposits from the public. Unlike commercial banks, they are not subject to regulation. Money-market funds are usually used by investors for the deposit of short-term funds, awaiting the time for when they might use it for purchasing other types of securities. Small businesses use the money market to deposit available short-term funds that earn a small rate of interest.

Large businesses usually park their excess funds by buying commercial papers. If and when they sell a CP to borrow, they may sell it directly to a money market fund or also through the CP market.

Small businesses only buy commercial paper. Big business both buys and sells commercial paper. Selling enables them to borrow short-term funds. Small businesses cannot do this. They have to borrow from a commercial bank or a finance company.

In the twenty years prior to 2006, interest rates were so low that four banks were looking for non-traditional ways to raise their profit levels because of deregulation of the sector. The short-term fund market is huge, and Citibank (or Citigroup) came up with the idea of structured investment vehicles (SIVs). [9] A traditional fixed-income paper has a single maturity and a single borrower, just as with mortgages. SIVs were a type of structured product. They invested in asset-backed securities as well as some financial corporate bonds, and the SIVs were the asset backing of commercial paper used to fund the purchased securities. Different mortgage notes or bonds with different maturity dates are known as collateralized debt obligation or asset backed securities. So an SIV might have real estate mortgages, car loans, and student loans. None of these mortgages or loans was individually evaluated by the SIV-issuing bank. The original mortgage lenders only use the simple standard of individual credit scores, otherwise known as FICO. It was the rating agencies like Moodys, Fitch, and S&P, that did the ratings on the SIVs. The various borrowers, via mortgages and loans, however, were not adequately rated by the bank or company selling bonds to the SIVs. The SIVs thought the use of complex mathematical models by the rating agencies for the CDs would be sufficient.

Today, after the huge losses in the values of SIVs, there are none known in existence. They were recorded "off balance sheet" because they were not subject to guidelines or regulation. These consequently did not reveal to the board of directors of the banks and mortgage lenders, such as Countrywide, the extent of the risks undertaken by them. The risks, including the liquidity risks to them, were very much underestimated and not even in the consciousness of most of top management, the government, and the private sector.

SIVs were an operation of issuing short-term commercial papers which were backed by CDOs. These CDOs were either asset-backed securities (ABS) or mortgage-based securities. The ABS were bundles of mortgage loans, car loans, and student loans. The mortgage-based securities were real estate mortgage loans.

These structures, coupled with bad vision in the measurement of risk, brought on the ensuing financial crisis on such a scale that it has caused an economic impact almost as great as the Great Depression. Only the better perspective of the application of monetary policy by the Fed averted a catastrophe.

These mathematical models were based on past performance indicators of the various securities within the SIVs, plus certain assumptions. Assumptions, however, still require judgment by perceptive people. Therein lies the rub. Judgment requires assigning probabilities, and accuracy can vary from one person's view to the next person's view.

The fundamentals of credit and collection state that the four "C's" are required for sound credit. These are: character of the borrower, adequate collateral for the loan, capacity to repay, and favorable business and economic conditions.

A joke that circulated during the bubble years was that many borrowers had no income, no job, no assets, and were otherwise known as "ninjas." However, the basic assumption of the lenders was that the prices of housing were going to rise at rates above the rates of interest. This would enable borrowers to refinance and even have extra housing value for home equity loans. These were the kinds of credit factors which were not integrated into the mathematical models.

Substantial numbers of mortgage loans were issued without collateral. These made "liar" loans and other sub-prime and near-prime loans possible. The sub-prime and near-prime loans may have had incomes, but those were insufficient to repay even just the interest because the ARM's interest rate would rise with an increase in the Fed fund rate. The Fed fund rates were raised from one percent on June 25, 2003 to 5.25 percent on June 29, 2006. [10] The Fed did this to contain asset inflation that was the result of speculation. The rise in interest rates would have been possible if housing prices had not reached its peak at the end of the third quarter of 2006. This was primarily because most speculators had already stopped buying property. The numbers of people who wanted to own homes (but not speculate) could no longer afford them, given the high prices and their insufficient incomes. The opportunities for speculators to "flip" property had virtually disappeared. Flipping meant buying a property through a no-collateral ARM and selling it within a very, very short period of time.

Early in 2005, I found out that some developers had stopped selling properties on credit to those with an existing mortgage. So the developers allowed speculators to buy on the condition that they could not resell within at least one year of the date of purchase. Many developers, too, by 2005, were adding more expensive features without increasing the new home price. All these events reduced the volume of total real estate transactions to very low levels. Prices dropped as speculators sought to cash in their paper profits. As losses of speculators started on low home prices, rates of delinquencies and foreclosures started to rise above historical rates.

The assumption that ever-rising housing prices would keep foreclosures at low levels was evidently flawed. The assumption was made based on the conclusion that the capacity to repay was favorable.

The fourth criterion for the extension of credit to borrowers is that conditions in the economy would be favorable. The conclusion that the favorable conditions that existed in the economy would remain steady or even become more favorable was accepted by a large majority in the financial sector. Otherwise, they would not have arrived at the ratings given to mortgages, as well as other debt instruments.

It seems almost unbelievable, even ridiculous, that the financial sector were mostly great believers in the assumptions contained in the mathematical models. These models were prepared by hired Ph.D.s in mathematics and sciences of Wall Street and by three rating agencies.

The assumption that housing buyers would be honest about their finances and be sensible (rather than credulous) must have been assumed in the mathematical models that led large numbers of financial institutions to invest in mortgage loans. I say that housing buyers, especially speculators, were wrong to believe that real estate would continuously increase in price. They also believed that relatively large fortunes could be made by buying houses for resale without a dime of capital infusion, and that this condition would prevail over time.

The Fed, as well as the rest of the financial sector, was mostly unaware that the substantial increase in total wealth of investors was due to asset inflation. Asset inflation would prove disastrous to the economy. The common perception, propagated by economists, was that increasing wealth would keep consumer spending levels rising. Increasing levels of consumption was considered good for the economy, for it made up for the increasing high rates of consumer indebtedness. Most consumers were indebted beyond what they could comfortably hope to repay. Most relied on increasing home prices that would enable them to acquire more equity loans.

Asset inflation in the real-estate markets meant that property prices and average medium and long-term interest rates were unrealistically high. The property could not be afforded even by those with the annual net income of median wage earners. That meant that the great majority of wage earners could not afford to repay. Most payments for principal amortizations were being achieved by borrowers from rising home equity loans. Property equity loans, as well as credit card loans, provided for a consumption level beyond their real wage incomes.

Asset inflation in financial securities means that the rise in general levels of security prices is not commensurate to the risks. The rates of return on these securities are lower relative to the risks and probable rates of future returns. In other words, price/earning multiples are too high, relative to risks.

Medium and long-run asset rates of return are dependent on increasing "real" incomes of consumers on the basis of a well-balanced economy and its resulting financial structure. If large numbers of highly leveraged business institutions have total net borrowings; if consumers, as a whole, have high levels of debt so as to produce a negligible total personal savings rate; and if the government also possesses high levels of debt relative to its tax revenues and is on high deficit levels, then inflation will surface. The outcome is reduced real incomes of consumers as measured in terms of reduced purchasing power and will correspondingly make housing unaffordable to current buyers or renters. Rental prices rise and fall depending on the direction of housing prices.

When the Fed became aware of the threat of asset inflation, they realized it was raising the cost of living. They therefore began to raise interest rates. They also began incorporating asset inflation rates in the CPI (Consumer Price Index).

Most consumers were indebted beyond what they could comfortably hope to repay. Most relied on increasing home prices that would enable them to acquire home equity loans. They were using their homes as ATMs.

The rise in interest rates was as fatal to the assets of speculators as thrust of a bullfighter's sword to a bull. It virtually ended all speculative activity. Almost every speculator lost all their housing assets and more, for they could still be pursued by the lenders who foreclosed or sold "short sales"—house sales owned by delinquent home owners at current market prices. These short sales enable the selling homeowner to get a less unfavorable credit rating than a foreclosed property homeowner.

The impact of losses on foreclosures, short sales, and delinquencies was dramatic for the financial institutions. By the end of the third quarter of 2008, consumers started cutting back on their consumption levels, but even with the continuously falling home prices since 2006, consumers were still spending at ever-higher levels until the third quarter of 2008. Credit card loans and car loans were still increasing at continuously higher levels at the end of the third quarter, and began to cut expenditures substantially. Many credit card and auto loans became delinquent. In the fourth quarter, employers started laying off employees and cutting down on overtime work. All these resulted in the worldwide financial crisis (or crises).

The financial sector functions as financial intermediaries. They serve the investors and the issuers of financial securities. Then there are the three rating agencies that rate the fixed-income securities according to their levels of risks.

The financial intermediaries are composed of the regulated commercial and savings banks and the unregulated shadow banking institutions such as investment banks and hedge funds. Also, there are the local government institutions, who issued municipal bonds as "auction rate bonds." "Tender option" bonds are like auction rate bonds offered by banks and some hedge funds and are backed by variable interest rate municipal bonds which mature usually within seven to fourteen days. The tender option bondholder is given the option to hold, sell, or repurchase at a lower rate of interest. The rate of interest after the maturity date is through an auction process. These variable rates of securities disappeared when the financial crisis began. Liquidity of these types of securities came to a standstill and effective short-term interest rates on them rose to as high as twenty percent.

The other financial intermediaries are money market funds that guarantee a redemption price of $1 for every $1 invested in the fund, plus the interest rate earned from its investments in government bills or private sector commercial papers. These CPs usually mature within a range from 30 days to one year. Then there are the pension funds, insurance companies, mutual funds, finance companies, and mortgage loan lenders other than the banks and secondary market institutions. The stock exchanges are for trading in equities and fixed-income securities. Secondary market institutions that trade derivatives are also exchanges. Over the counter (OTC) market is so called because it is for trades in all kinds of unlisted securities. There are a very few private, large, individual "wealth managers" outside of the banks, known as portfolio managers. The government-sponsored tertiary real estate mortgage markets are composed of Fannie Mae, Freddie Mac and Ginnie Mae. Then there are the other government-sponsored financial intermediaries for student loans and farm loans.

All of these financial intermediaries comprise the financial sector. These institutions are responsible for financial resource allocation to the rest of the economy.

The regulated institutions are the commercial and savings banks. They take savings and checking deposits from individuals, checking deposits from business, provide loans mainly to individuals and small and medium sized businesses, and finance foreign trade. Loans to individuals are known as consumer credit. These can take the form of short-term credit card financing, real estate mortgage finance, car loans, durable goods loans, and student loans.

The banks usually also have an investments management operation which is mainly involved in portfolio management. That includes a money market fund and other liquid common-funds facilities for investors, including various types of mutual funds and unit trust.

The unregulated (shadow) institutions are usually composed of investment banks and hedge funds. The investment banks engage in money market operations that buy and sell short-term securities of large corporations known as CPs, secondary market operations like brokerage facilities for equities and bonds, derivatives either through the stock and derivatives exchanges, and the over-the-counter markets.

The entire financial sector is essentially engaged in 1) money lending, 2) securities trading, 3) investment management, 4) arbitrage, 5) mergers and acquisitions. Sometimes hedge funds engage in a sixth activity, which is speculation.

The money lenders are the banks and finance companies. They are highly regulated, leveraged operations that borrow money as much as ten times their capital. The finance companies are unregulated unlike the commercial and savings banks. The Fed regulates their capital to loan ratios and makes certain that their reports on outstanding losses and delinquencies are timely and accurate. The banks insure depositors' money with the Federal Deposit Insurance Corporation (FDIC). The maximum amount of deposit guaranteed is decided by the government.

All the other institutions are virtually unregulated.

Booms and busts and financial disasters are a recurring feature in the financial system, mainly because finance requires a very perceptive, analytical, and quick mind. Two elements make the financial sector more fragile than other sectors of the economy. First, their activities require the reliable measurement of risks, and second, their operations are highly leveraged. It is only investment management activities that are not leveraged. It does, however, require a perceptive mind as well as character traits such as patience and self-control.

Arbitraging may seem less risky, even though it is a highly leveraged operation as well; they hedge their risks exposures. The hedge funds are primarily engaged in this activity. Most of their activities are in fixed-income securities.

The common arbitraging operation involves borrowing "short-term" money and lending "long-term" money and hedging the interest rate risk. Short-term money is usually cheaper or carries a smaller interest than long-term money. Short-term money loans are in the form of commercial paper and range in maturity dates from thirty days to one year. Long-term money loans usually come in the form of bonds and loans investments made by hedge funds. They make money by the "spread" or margin available from the lower borrowing costs and the higher interest income gained from long-term fixed-income securities.

Hedging is a technique designed to reduce or eliminate risks. It seeks to protect against the risk of loss in price or rate of interest fluctuations such as the price of corn or the value of an asset, such as a bond. It seeks to avoid loss through default or reduction or increase in interest rates, etc.

Hedging is done through securities called derivatives, which are highly leveraged securities. Securities trading is carried out mainly by investment banks, which underwrite equities and bond issues, mainly of corporations. This involves guaranteeing that the entire block of securities offered will be subscribed to. They also provide advice on mergers and acquisitions and underwrite the equity or loan-raising requirements of the acquirer. They also act as brokers and dealers in the stock and derivatives exchanges and in the over-the-counter markets.

In their trading operations, they may arbitrage securities listed on more than one exchange and take advantage of price differentials. They may also hedge some positions in their investments portfolios. They manage investments for small as well as for large investors, and they often take long or short positions on stocks, meaning they make more profits if the expectation of a rise in the prices of securities materializes. They may place a short sale on the expectation of a fall in the price of a particular security.

As the reader can see, the stability and dynamism of the financial sector requires people of sound judgment and high levels of education with a great capacity for applying one's knowledge. A strong sense of balance with regard to prudence, boldness, and self-control, as well as skills in selling and in maintaining personal relationships, is also essential.

The leveraging rate in the industry requires judgment and self-control. At times of high levels of economic activity, a financial institution needs to take more caution and reduce the leverage ratio as risks start to increase. Greed, fear, pride, and ambition are very hard to control where the possibility for huge gains exists side by side with the possibility for huge losses.

Derivatives are used by economic players who hedge to protect against a loss. Speculators are also preponderantly buyers and sellers of this form of security because it is highly leveraged and the possibility of huge returns exists. There is a great deal of participation in these markets, but few people fully grasp the risks inherent in these securities. For this reason, and the wide variations in liquidity existing over a short period of time, the risks for speculators are greater than in, say, the stock and bond markets. The risks are greater in the over-the-counter securities exchanges than in the futures exchanges.

The chart below shows the great price and liquidity variations in the commodities market over a relatively short period of time.

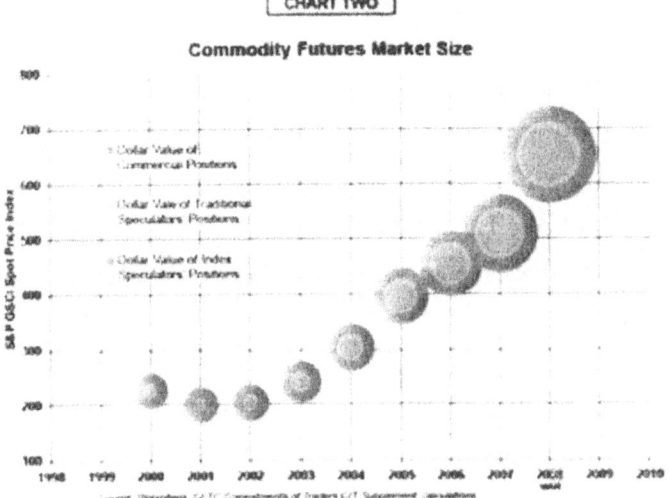

CHART TWO

Commodity Futures Market Size

COMMODITY FUTURES MARKET SIZE [11]

The potential for greater profits from speculation also implies the possibilities of greater risks attendant to excessive speculation in the derivatives markets. This is so because, as mentioned earlier, derivatives are leveraged securities. The price of the commodity, for example oil, could be so high that gasoline in many places was selling at $4 or more per gallon. This severely affected consumers and businesses as well as the price of food and other products.

Excessive speculation in derivatives may therefore severely impact the economy. That was what Warren Buffett must have meant when he said that derivatives were "weapons of mass destruction." For as our illustration above shows, the relatively short-run impact of derivatives speculation can increase prices of oil substantially. The price should reflect the fundamental demand and supply conditions for oil rather than being determined by the pressure of speculative activities.

The price of oil increasing to more than $140 a barrel was one of the major contributing factors that led to the financial crisis in 2008 and the present unpleasant economic conditions as of early 2010.

The degree of leveraging is relative to the ratio between borrowings and one's net equity position. It is also relative between one's income and one's borrowings.

The debt service ratio is between one's net cash inflows and one's net cash outflows. Whether one's debt service ratio is high or low risk, or a ratio level, which frees one from the threat of bankruptcy, depends on the accuracy of one's measurement of risk taken.

As we know, the measurement of risk is highly dependent on an individual's state of awareness of reality. This implies possession of vision or perception not colored by greed, lust for money or power, or pride or ambition, with the discipline to always reflect before engaging in any major financial commitment.

The high degree of leveraging by consumers and many businesses alike caused the financial crisis. The result is the present rate of unemployment and low incomes for the underemployed, and for the millions who depend basically on commissions and tips.

While there is a lot of noise in the economy that encourage people to keep up their high spirits, there is still no certainty that economic conditions will significantly improve even within one or two years. In later chapters, we will discuss the various factors that would enable the economy to materially improve, including the possibility of relieving the severe financial condition of nearly 50 percent of the workforce and many businesses.

The people who make decisions on their personal or business investment and other financial portfolios can therefore perceive better under the present circumstances. They can better perceive their own real set of values and the causes of their financial condition. This they can do after reading the succeeding chapters.

If those in a presently regrettable financial condition reflect honestly on their shortcomings, they will have a better chance of recovery, and sooner than others. If those in very challenging financial situations depend entirely upon others to deliver them from their circumstances, they will be highly disappointed.

The present economic environment requires a higher level of adaptive capability on the part both of leaders and the people. An unchanged set of values in the future will leave the economy as underproductive as it is today. Of course, people must conform to that better set of truly positive and constructive values, which are acquired and applied consistently over time.

Given human nature, and given the evidence recently of the inherent risks in forecasting and measuring potential risks and return, regulation is called for. Contingent liabilities must be prominently stated in annual and semi-annual reports.

Due to historical accounting practices that govern the preparation of financial statements, contingent liabilities are not stated in the balance sheet. They are considered as off balance sheet items. Enron worked this way. They guaranteed liabilities undertaken by others from profitable transactions with them that were recorded as contingent liabilities and therefore not recorded in the balance sheet. These were high risk liabilities that provided profitable transactions but fooled the public to the extent of Enron's liabilities. In the case of the banks, the structured investment vehicles were essentially short-term commercial papers, issued by the banks to be backed by complex securities known as CDOs. Because the buyers of the commercial paper blindly accepted the ratings of the ratings agencies, plus the guarantees of the issuing bank, the volume of the transactions were great. Eventually, when the quality of the CDOs deteriorated sharply, it brought the collapse of Lehman Bros. and the near total collapse of Merrill Lynch and Countrywide Mortgage Lenders. As mentioned earlier, no SIVs are known to exist today.

The inherent difficulties involved in the measurement of risk and probable returns should tell the investor that an institutional portfolio manager or the ordinary individual investor should use a great deal of caution when making decisions.

History tells us that people who call for restraint in times of excess are often not listened to. In some cases, they are ridiculed. People calling for outright change are usually vigorously opposed.

Such is the case in the financial markets where so many seek excessively large returns with comparatively little effort. The rumors—the talk otherwise called "noise" by professional investors—should not be a basis for investment decisions. But the fact is, people "hear" this advice without really listening, as the sixties song, "The Sounds of Silence," told us.

Civilizations depend on institutions to serve the common good. This must be achieved by a balance between the need of our business enterprises to remain strong, adaptable, and dynamic, and the need to serve all of stake holders' interests. This implies the importance of the exercise of corporate responsibility of management to all stake holders. For non-profits, it implies too, a greater responsibility to make certain there is no waste in its spending stream. After all, they get their revenue from donors and are not subject to the competitive pressures on business enterprise.

Today, regulations are being brought to bear mainly upon private financial institutions. The financial institutions complain about regulation. However, they must realize that whether it was bad judgment or disregard for high moral standards in their conduct, it is imperative that they conform to these high standards. The public expects financial markets to be sound within the borders of human capabilities at this stage of awareness and education of the population.

[9]   http//www.en.wikipedia.org/wiki/ structuredinvestmentvehicles

[10]   U.S.A. Historical Fed Fund Rates 2003 – 2005 The Federal Reserve Board

[11]   Source: Howestreet.com/articles

CHAPTER 5

THE AGRICULTURAL SECTOR

The importance of the agricultural sector to the economic and political security of the average American cannot be overstressed.

We have a highly diversified population with people from almost every country in the world. They generally favor their own cuisines, and most Americans have also enjoyed these cuisines as part of their dining out. Therefore, the availability and affordability of food from within as well as from without our borders is of vital importance to Americans.

Because the U.S. currency is convertible to virtually any foreign currency, the availability of food is not a major concern in the foreseeable future. We both import and export substantial amounts of food from all parts of the world. Our substantial productive and competitive capacity for food enables us to export substantially greater amounts than the amount we spend on imports.

The affordability of food is generally dependent on incomes and tastes. Some items are less expensive than others. Income levels, though, mostly determine the degree of food security of an individual and family unit. Overall, the median American household spent 12.6 percent of their wage incomes on food. [12] In 2006, households with incomes in the lowest reported income category spent 17.1 percent of their income on food, while those with incomes greater than $70,000 per annum spent 11.3 percent of income. [13] As is obvious, food inflation, as well as the overall inflation rate, is highly important to low-income groups. Given today's employment and unemployment scenario, any degree of inflation will be acutely felt by large numbers of unemployed and underemployed as wells as those working at the minimum wage level. The government food stamps program and other food aid programs of non-profits seek to mitigate food insecurity.

Another important consideration is the impact of agricultural food commodities on total jobs available in the economy. Increased agricultural production also contributes to other economic benefits from American food trade surpluses. The surplus enables us to reduce the overall trade deficit that we have been experiencing over the years. This is very important today, as our trade deficits have made us the world's largest debtor nation. This foreign debt size makes us poorer in many ways. Firstly, it causes some upward pressures on asset prices (asset inflation) when foreigners buy into our stock and bond markets. This makes us less competitive. Secondly, our interest bill from foreign dollar holders alone amounts to substantial sums of money given our foreign debt which amounts to over $3.9 trillion as of May 2010. [14]

The direct and indirect benefits of food production that we have mentioned are substantial. In 2008, the $115.2 billion of U.S. agricultural exports alone generated an additional

$157.2 billion in economic activity. [15] Farmers' purchases of fuel, fertilizer, and other inputs such as equipment spurred economic activity in the manufacturing, trade, and transportation sections. From agricultural exports alone, we gain a value from supporting economic activities surpassing $100 billion annually. In 2008, agricultural exports generated 920,000 full-time civilian jobs, including 608,000 jobs in the non-farm sector. [15]

The jobs in the non-farm sector were involved in assembly, processing, distributing, and servicing agricultural products. About 110,000 were in food processing, 197,000 were in trade and transportation, 65,000 were in other manufacturing sectors, and 237,000 were in other services. [15] Since total agricultural output in 2008 was more than $400 billion, one can realize that the total number of jobs created is substantially greater than the numbers employed by the farm sector.

On March 18, 2010, President Obama announced an export initiative that will help farmers and small businesses increase their exports. [16] This export initiative is expected to generate and support two million additional jobs. The announcement did not say what percentage of exports is projected for additional agricultural exports.

Land devoted to agriculture covers approximately 20 percent of the total land area of America. [17] Our total output is one of the largest and most productive agricultural sectors in the world. In fact, we have increased output substantially since 1947, while devoting the same amount of land to farming. This has been made possible through technological improvements. Productivity rates are higher in agriculture than in any other industry. The rate of increase in output is such that we continuously seek to develop our export markets.

We have the least number of people, relative to total population, dedicated to supplying a very large domestic and foreign market. We also export more food and food products than any other country. In spite of this, we are also one of the largest food importers. However, we still have a large net surplus in excess of food imports. Total agricultural output value currently amounts to over $400 billion, [17] and contributes approximately one percent to our GDP. [18] Ninety-eight percent are family owned, mostly small, farms. The proportion of large family and corporate owned farms is 10 percent of the total farms, [17] occupying 25 percent of total agricultural land, but producing 70 percent of the total farm output. Obviously, large farms are more productive. Small farms, as a rule, do not recover economic costs such as unpaid labor from revenues. However, other incomes from non-farm activities and passive incomes enable households living on farms to have much higher average incomes. They also have greater wealth in the form of farm land than the average American household.

The Economic Research Service (ERS) of the Department of Agriculture tracks both the availability of food and its affordability. The availability measure they use does not consider demand factors like wastage at home, as well as the marketing system. It provides trends in consumption levels over time rather than absolute levels of food eaten. The availability index is constructed through annual calculations of the available supply of each commodity. It is the sum of production, plus beginning inventories and imports, less exports, farm, industrial, and end of the year inventories. This, then, is the estimated amount of food available for consumption. "The data reveal how the sometimes conflicting and sometimes reinforcing political, economic, and social forces affect the types and amounts of commodities available for consumption." [19] Growing global food sources and markets, rising incomes, availability of health information, new technologies, agricultural policies, and changing social norms, all impact the types and volumes of commodities available for consumption.

Over the past century, Americans have consumed more processed foods, including fruits. Today, processed convenience foods account for 49 percent of total food consumption. [19] This, for example, reveals also trends indicating the potential for pleasurable and healthy diets for Americans. The data has shown that supplies are more than adequate relative to the average 2,000-calorie diet for grains and meats. The data of total supplies available have shown that supplies are more than adequate for healthy living needs. However, vegetables, dairy, and fruits were inadequate relative to dietary recommendations. It would seem from all the above that the needed availability can be secured if the actual demand existed. However, habits and our present set of nutritional values, income streams, and spending values govern the final demand.

The affordability of food is a function of net incomes and taste. The importance people attach to recommended healthy living standards for various types of food also governs consumption. Food consumption, as a percentage of disposable income, may reveal values for various types of consumer expenditures such as food, shelter, luxuries, and savings. Some health conditions arise, not just from inherited physical, structural tendencies like height, genes, weight, etc., but from environmental factors and the responses of individuals to them.

Today, obesity is a major concern of leaders and citizens alike, for obesity translates into higher health care costs. Health care, at present, is unaffordable to large numbers of the population. Since enterprise must carry most of the health insurance burden, an impact is felt in the competitiveness of American enterprise and workers.

The chart below shows the imbalance between the loss-adjusted per-capita food availability and the dietary recommendations in 2008. [(20

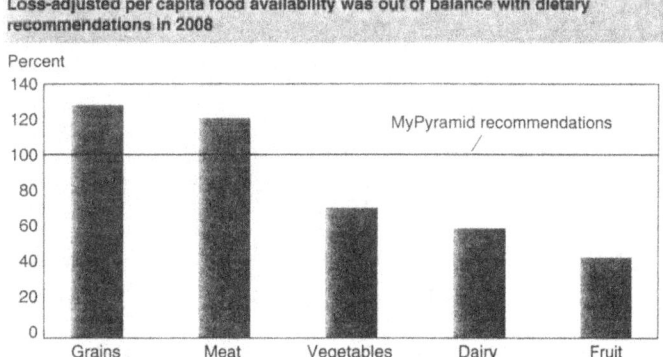

Loss-adjusted per capita food availability was out of balance with dietary recommendations in 2008

Based on a 2,000-calorie diet. Loss-adjusted food availability data are a proxy for consumption. Source: USDA, Economic Research Service, Food Availability (Per Capita) Data System.

Loss Adjusted Per capita food Availability
Was Out Of Balance with Dietary
Recommendations in 2008
USDA Economic Research for Service Food
Availability (per capita) Data System.

The consumption patterns among beef, pork, chicken, and turkey are reflected in the chart below, [(21)] which uses the food availability data. The increasing per-capita consumption of chicken and turkey since 1980 is due to perception that they are healthier meats, with a lower fat content than beef and pork.

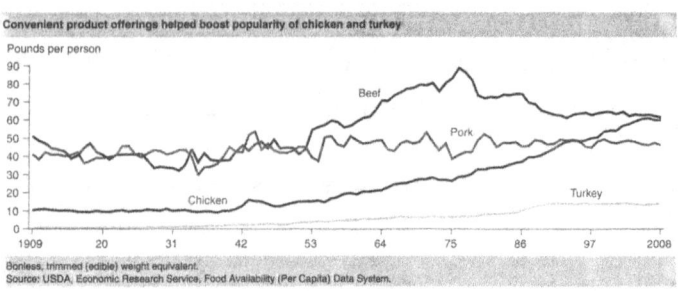

Convenient Product Offerings helped
Popularity of Chicken and Turkey

Source: USDA Economic Research Service
Food Availability (per capita) Data System.

The increasing size of food servings over
the years, especially when eating out, reflects
the use of a marketing tool to gain customers
and the tendency of Americans to eat more.
It may be that eating more of an imbalanced
or unhealthy diet is a reflection of increasing
tension felt by average Americans due to economic, financial, and social pressures.

The various factors that impact our competitiveness are a major concern for leaders and
citizens. The state of our mental and physical
health is of great importance. Many people
today realize more than ever the intercon-
nectedness of the mental and physical states

of well-being. There is increasing awareness of the need for healthy diets, but as the data above shows, large segments of the population do not have healthy eating habits. This, along with a lack of exercise and a greater number of people leading sedentary lives, leads to obesity and related medical diseases and conditions. For many unhealthy individuals, obesity is prevalent in low income groups and led to a study [19] by social leaders as to whether it was caused by the food stamps aid program.

Food stamps, designed to help low-income groups maintain basic nutritional needs, were received by 24 million people in 2004. [19] The study looked also at the possibility that replenishment of the food stamp aid card is usually done at the end of each month. The thinking was that recipients would binge at the replenishment and go hungry towards the end of the month. Comparisons between non-aid participants in the low income groups did not reveal any substantive conclusion. [19] The non-aid participant, however, had less obesity problems.

Today, at the end of the first quarter of 2010, the total numbers of unemployed, those working part-time, plus those whose gratuities or commission incomes have fallen dramatically, I calculate to number over 50 million. [22] These conditions may render many of these people in need of food stamps aid and other welfare programs. The cost to the taxpayer will be substantial. The budget deficits could cause inflation. This, in turn, could increase welfare needs.

Unless these issues of obesity and rates of high unemployment and underemployment are resolved, health conditions will deteriorate further. It is most unlikely that food prices will fall. A little later, this conclusion will be arrived at from an explanation of conditions in the agricultural sector.

All these factors contribute to the possibility that, if the present state of affairs continues, America may become a third-world country. The economic problems, such as shortages of educated workers and surpluses of unskilled workers due to social conditions, could escalate. As is well know, the quality of education (and the "quality" of students) has deteriorated. The consciousness of healthy living standards seem to improve, but is not given serious considerations by substantial numbers of people.

Present-day labor conditions for hired farm workers (supervisors and managers excepted) reveal that they are mostly uneducated and that they and their families are large recipients of economic (welfare) assistance. [17] Most hired farm workers are uneducated and classified as regular or migratory farm workers. The migratory workers work per season. Substantial numbers of this seasonal workforce are Hispanics. The majority of farm workers, however, are whites. Most migratory workers are from Mexico, and come for the season, at the end of which they return to their homes across the border. [17]

Most hired farm workers are employed by large farms. The majority of farm workers reveal a younger workforce. The small farms reveal a substantial number of workers aged 65 and older (as owners) without a younger generation ready to take over. These conditions, plus a lack of adequate profitability for most small farms, have forced them to sell their properties. These conditions have contributed to structural shifts which have raised the share of the large and very large farms of aggregate agricultural production in the United States. There are still many small farms that are profitable; however, there are economies of scale which enable large farms to be more productive and profitable. The numbers employed in the farm sector have substantially decreased over the past five decades. Greater productivity brought about by increased efficiency and technology has enabled the farm sector to reduce its hired workers from 3.4 million in 1960 to a little over 1 million as of the first quarter of 2010. [17]

Immigration issues today are such that sometimes the lack of migratory workers from Mexico has meant a serious shortage of workers. This has, at times, resulted in unharvested produce such as fruits.

Productivity decline, coupled with higher medical and health insurance costs, will result in lower real incomes. It is most likely that the burden of medical insurance over time will fall more heavily upon the American worker to maintain the competitiveness of enterprise.

The response of the American worker to the increasing reduction of improvement rates of productivity will very much govern the future of the economy.

Physical health is an issue of serious concern.

A reduction in meat and grains, and a substantial increase in dairy, vegetables, and fruit consumption, will mean higher absolute spending for food. The relative prices for total requirements of the various types of food are higher for dairy, vegetables, and fruits.

The numbers of workers in agriculture and related industries are at present only about 2.5 million. [22] The output, however, allows a much greater number of workers in the food processing, packaging, and marketing sectors as well as in various industrial uses of food commodities. Corn, for example, has industrial uses other than biofuels. The food-service sector, comprising supply chains, restaurants, fast food chains, and canteens, employs one of the highest numbers of like workers in the economy. [23]

The total value of net exports to our balance of trade is also an important positive contribution to the competitiveness of the American enterprise. The impact of the balance of trade and services on the overall financial strength and vitality of the economy is substantial.

The numbers of people employed in food service and preparation total approximately five million. [23] Full-dining service comprises 60 percent of the restaurant industry. Full-dining service workers earn tips that enable them to live comfortably above the minimum wage workers who work without gratuities.

Over the past 10 years, food imports have grown substantially to $71.7 billion in calendar year 2009. [24] Most food imports are for products for which America has inadequate resources for meeting demand. These are mainly products such as seafood, coffee, bananas, and other tropical processed and unprocessed foods. Imports of off-season temperate-zone produce are also substantial. Some imported food products are cheaper than locally produced ones, so this also is an important factor. As a rule, American agriculture is competitive, and cheaper imports are generally for less fastidious consumers.

The following chart reflects the percentage share of import of total consumption based on values. Import shares, based on values, are highest for seafood, fish, sugar, and confections in 2005.

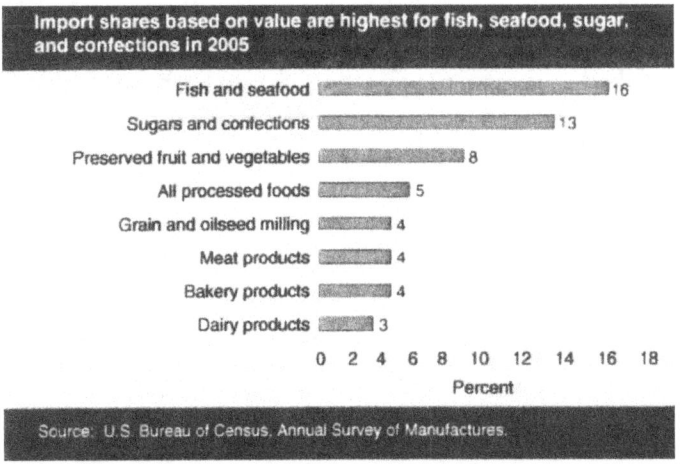

Import Shares based on Value are Highest for Fish, Seafood. Sugar and Confections in 2005
Source: U.S. Bureau of Census Annual Survey of Manufactures
http://www.ers.usda.gov/amberwaves/ March 2010/data

Food imports have been stable and rising over the years, reflecting in part changes in tastes due to ethnic diversity and changes in real incomes.

Exports, however, have been more erratic. Exports declined in 1997–99 due to reduced demand caused by the global financial crisis which started in Asia but food exports kept growing to $115 billion in 2008. [24] The world economic slowdown, which started in the fourth quarter of 2008, brought a decline in global consumption, trade, and prices, which reduced exports in 2009.

Xcyhvpbulk.xls
Bulk = wheat, rice, feed grains, soybeans (& other oilseeds), cotton & linters, and tobacco
Calendar year = January-December

Calendar year bulk and high-value agricultural product exports

	BULK sum *	HVP calc *	Total Ag Exports million U.S. $	Bulk #2**	HVP #2**
CY1976	15,782	7,196	22,978	16,052	6,926
CY1977	15,317	8,319	23,636	15,752	7,884
CY1978	19,442	9,940	29,382	20,140	9,242
CY1979	22,965	11,784	34,749	23,517	11,232
CY1980	27,538	13,696	41,234	28,109	13,126
CY1981	28,700	14,637	43,338	29,332	14,006
CY1982	23,862	12,765	36,627	24,386	12,241
CY1983	23,635	12,464	36,099	23,982	12,117
CY1984	24,814	12,990	37,804	25,467	12,337
CY1985	17,199	11,843	29,041	17,503	11,539
CY1986	13,120	13,102	26,222	13,342	12,880
CY1987	14,573	14,136	28,709	14,783	13,926
CY1988	19,708	17,372	37,080	19,946	17,135
CY1989	22,125	17,978	40,103	22,469	17,634
CY1990	19,457	20,037	39,495	19,739	19,755
CY1991	17,666	21,720	39,386	18,032	21,354
CY1992	19,037	24,209	43,247	19,402	23,844
CY1993	17,938	25,034	42,972	18,269	24,703
CY1994	18,086	28,086	46,172	18,517	27,655
CY1995	25,094	31,112	56,206	25,624	30,582
CY1996	28,105	32,313	60,418	28,649	31,769
CY1997	22,807	34,342	57,149	23,703	33,445
CY1998	18,750	33,062	51,812	19,369	32,442
CY 1999	13,443	34,947	48,389	14,224	34,166
CY 2000	14,514	36,751	51,265	15,272	35,993
CY 2001	14,894	38,785	53,679	15,915	37,764
CY 2002	15,162	37,981	53,143	16,100	37,044
CY 2003	18,845	40,548	59,392	19,527	39,866
CY 2004	24,664	36,763	61,426	25,380	36,046
CY 2005	22,204	40,978	63,182	22,943	40,239
CY 2006	25,712	45,236	70,949	26,530	44,419
CY 2007	36,486	53,504	89,990	37,380	52,610
CY 2008	49,840	65,438	115,278	50,909	64,369
CY 2009	38,052	60,559	98,611	39,029	59,582

* Bulk including soybeans only; excludes other oilseeds.
**Bulk #2 includes all oilseeds.
history-2000 corrected for ERS/FAS code reconciliation on 12/18/00.
1990-2006 corrected for ERS/FAS code reconciliation of fall 2006.
Economic Research Service, USDA
updated 2/19/2010

Calendar Year and High-Value Agricultural Product Exports

mbulkhvpcy.xls

U.S. imports of bulk & high-value agricultural products, by calendar year

	Bulk	HVP	Total Imports	Bulk Share	HVP Share
	Million dollars			Percent	
1976	395	10,570	10,966	3.6%	96.4%
1977	425	13,016	13,441	3.2%	96.8%
1978	453	14,352	14,804	3.1%	96.9%
1979	507	16,217	16,723	3.0%	97.0%
1980	528	16,873	17,401	3.0%	97.0%
1981	921	15,986	16,907	5.4%	94.6%
1982	645	14,700	15,345	4.2%	95.8%
1983	911	15,625	16,536	5.5%	94.5%
1984	770	18,565	19,334	4.0%	96.0%
1985	819	19,149	19,968	4.1%	95.9%
1986	822	20,630	21,453	3.8%	96.2%
1987	829	19,574	20,402	4.1%	95.9%
1988	912	20,042	20,955	4.4%	95.6%
1989	1,070	20,809	21,879	4.9%	95.1%
1990	1,007	21,911	22,918	4.4%	95.6%
1991	1,151	21,724	22,875	5.0%	95.0%
1992	1,902	22,894	24,796	7.7%	92.3%
1993	2,038	23,079	25,117	8.1%	91.9%
1994	1,628	25,396	27,024	6.0%	94.0%
1995	1,426	28,829	30,255	4.7%	95.3%
1996	2,219	31,293	33,511	6.6%	93.4%
1997	2,362	33,786	36,148	6.5%	93.5%
1998	1,808	35,086	36,894	4.9%	95.1%
1999	1,790	35,883	37,673	4.8%	95.2%
2000	1,514	37,460	38,974	3.9%	96.1%
2001	1,638	37,728	39,366	4.2%	95.8%
2002	1,640	40,275	41,915	3.9%	96.1%
2003	1,566	45,818	47,384	3.3%	96.7%
2004	1,780	52,209	53,989	3.3%	96.7%
2005	1,701	57,590	59,291	2.9%	97.1%
2006	2,211	63,115	65,326	3.4%	96.6%
2007	2,991	68,922	71,913	4.2%	95.8%
2008	4,652	75,835	80,488	5.8%	94.2%
2009	3,490	68,209	71,699	4.9%	95.1%

Bulk = wheat, rice, coarse grains, all oilseeds, tobacco, cotton & linters.
HVP = all other imports; calculated as total imports minus bulk.
history-2000 corrected for ERS/FAS code reconciliation on 12/18/00.
1990-2006 corrected for ERS/FAS code reconciliation of fall 2006.
Economic Research Service, USDA
updated 2/19/2010

U. S. Imports of Bulk & High-Value Agricultural Products By Calendar Year

Top 15 U.S. agricultural export destinations, by calendar year, value $U.S.

Country	CY2009	Country	CY2008
World Total	98,611,239,808	World Total	115,277,565,384
1 Canada	15,701,171,599	Canada	16,253,364,409
2 China	13,149,770,080	Mexico	16,025,184,360
3 Mexico	12,946,198,277	Japan	13,223,117,873
4 Japan	11,117,097,198	China	12,114,771,880
5 European Union-27	7,460,500,172	European Union-27	10,080,401,452
6 South Korea	3,922,527,853	Korea, South	5,561,380,583
7 Taiwan	2,990,459,922	Taiwan	3,419,411,583
8 Hong Kong	2,051,045,597	Indonesia	2,194,977,199
9 Indonesia	1,797,020,267	Egypt	2,050,079,968
10 Turkey	1,499,307,134	Russia	1,838,140,790
11 Russia	1,441,072,118	Philippines	1,734,346,280
12 Egypt	1,354,465,706	Hong Kong	1,714,552,307
13 Philippines	1,293,618,073	Turkey	1,695,608,435
14 Thailand	1,046,925,982	Colombia	1,675,289,818
15 Venezuela	955,879,527	Venezuela	1,597,990,911

history-2000 corrected for ERS/FAS code reconciliation 12/18/00.
1999-2002 corrected for ERS/FAS errata application.
ERS/USDA.
Historic data revised to include European Union-27 2/25/08.
updated 2/19/2010.

Top 15 U.S. Agricultural Export Sources by Calendar Year, $U.S. Value

Top 15 U.S. agricultural import sources, by calendar year, $U.S. value

Country	CY 2009	Country	CY 2008
World Total	71,698,790,536	World Total	80,487,688,889
1 Canada	14,709,216,659	Canada	18,009,005,636
2 European Union-27	13,388,303,421	European Union-27	15,509,565,134
3 Mexico	11,380,410,503	Mexico	10,907,047,601
4 China	2,874,289,490	China	3,451,161,555
5 Brazil	2,435,400,913	Indonesia	2,815,496,408
6 Australia	2,318,291,227	Brazil	2,615,127,922
7 Chile	2,145,349,399	Australia	2,425,479,498
8 Indonesia	1,786,608,597	Chile	2,048,760,742
9 Colombia	1,769,478,753	Thailand	1,916,994,882
10 New Zealand	1,613,213,888	Malaysia	1,867,328,471
11 Thailand	1,566,748,556	New Zealand	1,833,202,093
12 Guatemala	1,298,334,564	Colombia	1,769,291,515
13 Malaysia	1,295,445,219	India	1,600,633,960
14 India	1,236,296,809	Guatemala	1,314,162,833
15 Costa Rica	1,092,510,724	Argentina	1,257,172,450

history-2000 corrected for ERS/FAS code reconciliation 12/18/00.   Canada
1999-2002 corrected for ERS/FAS errata application.
ERS/USDA.
Historic data revised to include European Union-27 2/25/08.
updated 2/19/2010.

Top U.S. Agricultural Import Sources by Calendar Year $U. S. Value

The tables above show import and export values over time. [25] The import figures reflected in calendar year (CY) 2000 and 2008 show the magnitude of increases in total imports. The annual export figures also manifest major increases from CY 2000 to 2009.

Over 60 percent of our imports come from just three countries—Canada, Mexico, and China—and the European Union. Since CY 2000, China has become a major source for food imports, which accounted for about $2.87 billion in 2008. However, our total food exports in dollars to China are about the same as imports. Exports-wise, Canada and Mexico are the leading U.S. trading partners, followed by Japan and, as of CY 2008, by China. These four nations buy 50 percent of U.S. food exports. Canada, Mexico, and the European Union supplied 55 percent of U.S. agricultural imports in 2008. [25]

In the 1990s, high value products (HVP) production expanded. In fiscal year 1991, HVP exports exceeded agricultural bulk products exports like wheat, rice, coarse grains, oilseeds, cotton, and tobacco. HVPs are meats, poultry, live animals, oilseed meals, vegetable oils, fruits, vegetables, dairy products, and beverages. Since 1991, HVP exports have continued to exceed bulk exports, even in years of overall decline in agricultural trade. [26] This expansion in relatively greater quantities of HVP versus bulk commodities is happening too, in our domestic markets, as people have diversified in their food tastes. More recent nutritional findings at this point also suggest that it is healthier to eat HV food products than just plain steaks and potatoes.

Opportunities in the agricultural sector for those with education and ability to do better than unskilled labor are plentiful. In the production of some HVP that do not require much capital but plenty of technical knowledge, such as in the growing of orchids or off-season vegetables, nurseries are reasonably abundant. Those majoring in biology certainly have great opportunities, either for high-paying stable jobs, or for their own business. This is a sector which is growing and will continue to grow. If you are more inclined to the commercial aspects of agricultural products for import and export, this will be a less crowded business to get into.

In this field of trading, formal education is not necessary. Some knowledge and experience in purchasing and the mechanics of importing and exporting is essentially all the basics you need. The most important skills are a knowledge of your products and a perceptive mind for trends and conditions in the various markets the business serves. All a small business aspirant needs is a mind that is perceptive and open to opportunities. The rest of the knowledge requirements you can hire.

At present, our costs of production in the agricultural sector enable us to compete in spite of our high wage rates. This is a product of a higher standard of living which has raised our costs of doing business. Our higher standard of living has been achieved by technological improvements, education, and other factors, and the corresponding productive levels have enabled us to expect higher wages and returns. Among the other factors which have given us one of the highest standards of living are an abundance of natural resources and a relatively smaller population vis-à-vis our productive lands. Also, from an observer's point of view, there seems to be a greater preponderance in our society of people with entrepreneurial, research, and development capabilities as well as managerial talents. American culture, too, encourages the full exploitation of its people's education and talents.

Our cost of production is still competitive, in spite of our high wages, because our labor productivity is still much greater than, say, China or Brazil and Argentina. Within five years, in my opinion, we will be able to maintain our competitiveness and our current surplus in this sector. This is only qualified by the possibility of unintended consequences in new government policies and in entrepreneurial and managerial decisions. There are also many other possible political, economic, and social responses to the adverse economic conditions obtaining in our country that could negatively impact our competitiveness. However, without being overly optimistic, we can expect the growth in agricultural incomes to continue within the next five years. By the end of this book, you should be able to judge for yourself whether the author's opinions are overly optimistic or pessimistic.

The opportunities in the horticultural field is, in fact, corroborated by many and growing numbers of the well-to-do who are in the process of retiring and moving to small towns for part-time engagement in this business. Many, who are fully retired, have also engaged part-time in this endeavor. Most HVPs do not require much labor time. Even in poultry-raising today, it does not need large capital or full-time labor. Yet, they are more rewarding financially. The field requires more knowledge than traditional small farming.

Dairy farming today requires larger farms and new management know-how for the more profitable areas of organically produced milk and cheeses. Agriculture and aquaculture, and even fishing enterprises and ranching lend themselves to family ownership rather than a true corporate entity. Corporations that are engaged in hog-raising usually do so as both a market for their more profitable feed products business as well as their main line. They may even cater to large numbers of independent hog-raising farms with breeders and feed and veterinary products.

The corporate sector is doing more direct-contract negotiations with farmers instead of going through the cash "open" markets for their food processing and distribution operations. This is especially true in the poultry and livestock industries. This enables them to lower costs by reducing the numbers in the supply chain.

In the author's opinion, these sectors are secure against foreign competition within the next five years.

[12]   U.S. Department of Labor, Bureau of Labor Statistics, "Consumer Expenditure Survey." 2007

[13]   ERS/USDA Food and Expenditures 2007

[14]   The Department of the Treasury/Federal Reserve Board

[15]   ERS/USA Data – Agricultural Trade Multipliers-effects of the Trade on the U.S. Economy.

[16]   U.S. Department of State: Economic, Energy, Agricultural, and Trade Issues "Stimulating Global Economic Growth through U.S. Exports" March 18, 2010.

[17]   ERS/USDA Economic Information Bulletin No. 63 February 2010/"Small Farms in the United States/ Persistence Under Pressure"

[18]   Annual Industry Accounts bea.gov/industry

[19]   ERS/USDA Amber Waves Magazine March 2010/Data Feature/

[20]   Based on a 2,000-calorie diet. Loss adjusted food availability data are a proxy for consumption.

(21) Department of Agriculture, "Tracking a Century of American Eating." Amber Magazine (February 2008). This is the loss-adjusted data for spoilage and wastage translated into daily per-capita calories and food servings.

(22) Bureau of Labor Statistics Total Employed Persons by Class of Workers and Part-time Status

(23) Bureau of Labor Statistics, Occupational Employment Statistic, Employment and Wages of the Largest Occupations, May 2008.

(24) ERS.USDA.gov Agricultural Exports and Imports by Calendar Year (2009)

(25) ERS.USDA.gov Agricultural Exports and Imports by Calendar Years 2000 – 2009

(26) ERS/USDA Amber Waves Magazine March 2010/Data Feature

CHAPTER 6

THE GOODS-PRODUCING SECTOR

Introduction

This chapter is designed to show the average reader, the size and variety of the industries and markets which our good-producing sector serves. The reader will see that we have lost sizeable domestic market share to imports. It also seeks to show which industries seem to be presently losing out to foreign competition. Over the years our manufacturing industries have sought a technological advantage as just about the only competitive tool left for them to use. The onslaught of inflation reduced savings rates of the population causing higher wages, high inflation rates for health care, and just about rendered us uncompetitive in labor intensive industries. It so happens that labor intensive industries employ the greatest number of workers. Thus we suffered a net loss of millions of manufacturing jobs to foreign competition. There have also been substantial losses of jobs due to productivity improvements. For this reason manufacturing jobs command the highest level of wages for the skilled worker.

Forestry and Logging

Industries in forestry and logging grow and harvest timber on a long production timetable, that is, 10 years or more. Long production cycles use different production processes than short production processes, which require more horticultural interventions prior to harvest. For these reasons, Christmas tree production and other production involving cycles of less than 10 years, are classified by the Bureau of Labor Statistics Office, in the Crop Production Subsector. [27]

Total employment in the forestry and logging industries as of 2008 totaled 40,320. It is a comparatively small subsector with only a total of 9,977 private industry establishments and 96 government owned as of the third quarter of 2009. It contracted in the number of private industry establishments from the fourth quarter of 2008, reflecting the decline in demand for housing lumber. Salary and wage levels were generally in the $33,000 to $34,000 per annum range for skilled workers as of 2008. Supervisors and managers, as of the same year, made around $57,000 per annum. [27] This subsector is an important supplier to the construction and paper industry, as well as the preservation of the environment. Employment numbers are sensitive to fluctuations in the economy, especially the construction and paper industries. These industries are one of the least threatened by foreign competition. It can, however, be cyclical in nature because construction is cyclical. The major growth source for construction is from recycling, but is confined by greater use of computers. Newsprint is the paper most affected by computers. Demand for other types of paper is still growing.

There doesn't seem to be any threat within the foreseeable future to the survival of the forestry and logging industries.

Mining, Quarrying, and Oil and Gas Extraction

The term mining here is used in the broad sense of quarrying, well operations, beneficiating (e.g. crushing, screening, washing, and flotation), and other preparations customarily performed at the mine site. Total employment in the industry numbered 651,300 as of March 10, 2010. [28] Its contribution of real value added to total GDP amounted to $110.5 billion. [29] Average earnings of all employees amounted to $27.98 per hour. [28]

Prices of these products fluctuate, sometimes daily. The producer price index [28] reflects as much as a 10 percent price movement between December 2009 and January 2010.

There were complaints by a group of mining companies in Nevada on television that we import as much as 50 percent of our mineral needs due to "bureaucratic red tape." They did not elaborate on that announcement. It is obviously a vital sector because oil imports alone make up at times nearly 50 percent of our trade deficit. There is some competition here developing from renewable energy,

energy-efficiency products, and energy conservation projects. However, it may take more than five years before we can hope to arrive at independence from imported oil. In mineral imports, there is no present threat of displacement. Coal is highly abundant in our country but its pollution impact causes concerns for the environment. It seems, however, that its displacement by other products or means is still a very long way away.

Demand for these subsectors' various products is sensitive to global economic conditions. Therefore, employment conditions are very volatile relative to the global economy. However, recently the government has enacted measures that will stimulate offshore oil and gas drilling. This will reduce the unemployment rate, but it will also have the result of substantially reducing our trade deficits if more oil and gas is found and produced. Unfortunately, the recent Gulf oil spill may stall (or kill) all these projects. Presently, all offshore drilling has been postponed for a period of six months.

A substantial reduction in our trade deficit would have resulted in much greater competitiveness of our enterprises vis-à-vis imports. For these reasons, primarily, the government is doing all it can to improve not only our environment but also to reduce our trade deficit and improve our economy's production-costs competitiveness. It is well to bear in mind that this will substantially help enterprise compete, not only in our own domestic markets but also in foreign or export markets—if we can keep energy costs stable and low.

Stable solid mineral ore prices will also improve our standard of living by keeping the costs of durable goods and housing lower. The size of the subsector's output and contribution to overall GDP may be relatively small but its importance to our economy must be emphasized. The rest of the economy will be hobbled by their shortage or high prices if either should occur.

Construction

The construction subsector is comprised of enterprises engaged in the construction of buildings or engineering projects (e.g., highways and utility systems). Included are establishments primarily engaged in subdividing land for sale as building sites. According to the Bureau of Labor Statistics classification, construction work may include new work, additions, alterations or maintenance and repairs. Work is done essentially by contractors or subcontractors. [30] Employment figures are large, numbering as many as 5,592,000 as of March 2010 despite the present economic recession. It is a highly cyclical industry and the present unemployment rate of 24.9 percent as of March 10, 2010 reflects this. [30] As of February 2010, job openings numbered 62,000 nationwide. There were 237,000 hires and 302,000 separations from work. Gross job gains in the second quarter of 2009 were 614,000. Gross job losses for the same period were 940,000. The Bureau of Labor Statistics on Industries, at a glance, reflects the construction industry's conditions and more. [30] Wages are high and skilled workers make substantially more than ordinary construction workers. It is mainly unionized. Total benefits are slightly more than 30 percent of total compensation. Wages and salaries amount to almost 70 percent. [30]

Since construction involves mainly the supply of labor, there are approximately 837,800 private industry establishments as of the third quarter of 2009. Local and state government-owned firms numbered 6,306. The federal government had three establishments in the construction industry as of the third quarter of 2009. [30]

Real value added by the construction industry contributed to $336.5 billion. It has fallen substantially from $418.5 billion in 2005 at about the peak of the construction boom. While its contribution to total GDP is only about 3.2 percent, it employs nearly five percent of the overall work force. [29]

As mentioned earlier, earnings are substantially more than the average hourly earnings overall in the goods-producing sector, and are eclipsed only by the manufacturing subsector average hourly earnings. Construction work average earnings are of course substantially more than the $18.50 average hourly wage of the whole workforce. Because of the high level of wages, this sector's recovery is important to the alleviation of present high levels of unemployment. Also, substantial dollar amounts of material inputs make it a highly important contributor to the economy.

The total value of business transacted amounted to $1.782 trillion as of 2007, at the peak of the construction boom that started mainly in 2002. Therefore, we can perceive its substantial impact on other industries, including the retail trade, since its value of business transacted is $5.12 per dollar of payroll. [31]

For investors in the equities market, and for those in government policy and the banking system, construction activity, as an economic indicator, is highly valued for its use for strategic and tactical measures to be undertaken by many players. While financing availability is critical to the construction industry, the level of wages and full employment are more critical to its level of activity. The last construction boom was triggered by low interest rates and unrealistic lending policies rather than a fundamental improvement in the level of wages and in the financial structure of the whole economy.

Manufacturing

Real value added by the manufacturing industry as of 2008 was $1.574 trillion. Durable goods contributed $1.061 trillion, while non-durables contributed $539.4 billion. [29]

In 2008, durable goods turned down for the first time since 2001. On the other hand, non-durable goods manufacturing contracted in five of the last 10 years. [32] If you will look on reference 5 of Table 4, you will see that our manufacturing cost competitiveness is diminishing. In durable-goods manufacturing we have technological advantages and transport-costs advantages for our domestic markets. In the non-durables, low manufacturing costs are highly vital to enable us to protect our domestic markets from continuously increasing imports, as well as capture foreign export markets. However, Japan, Korea, and Taiwan seem to out-compete us in motor vehicles and home appliances. China's low labor costs enable them to out-compete us in domestic and world markets in most non-durables other than food, beverage, and tobacco products, as well as chemical products.

We are the world's largest manufacturing economy. [32] A little over 11 million were employed as of March 2010. This was about nine percent of the overall workforce of 130,920,000 as of the end of 2009 or early January 2010. It is also a little above 10 percent of the private sector workforce of 107,056,000. [22]

We had lower manufacturing compensation costs than most European economies, Australia, the United Kingdom, and Canada. "Average costs in the United States were higher than in most countries covered outside of Europe." [33]

Manufacturing employment has fallen by 2.1 million in less than two years since December 2007. [33] In 2008, manufacturing's share of GDP fell to 11.5 percent, its lowest level since 1947. [31]

There are issues about our manufacturing sector, such as whether its share of GDP is sufficient to sustain the size and wage levels of the services sector. We need to produce more of the manufactured goods in the domestic economy or produce more for the export markets. If we do not make any effort in either direction, we will definitely become permanently a third-world country.

Let's face it, the economic conditions in the past two years have been so bad, it is only partially alleviated by huge budget deficits. Budget deficits generate spending which would subsequently create jobs. However, this deficit would just mean a greater foreign debt if not inflation. These would compound our problems. We have been, and are still selling, in reality, assets, if not claims, on our future income streams.

The problem of seeking growth through more exports of our high wage products produces a measure of instability because they are capital goods. Most of our manufactured exports practically depend on only a technological superiority. Unfortunately, we do not command any more markets in the light manufacturing consumer goods sector. We have conceded domestic and world markets to China in light manufacturing industries. Thus, we have large trade deficits. Foreign-made cars with almost no domestic content sell in huge numbers in our country. Many home appliances, with almost no domestic content, are also sold here. If the major durable goods industries cannot acquire sufficient economies of scale, then it will need to ship jobs overseas.

While cheaper goods from imports bring down the cost of living if substantial wage earners are without well-paying jobs, the whole exercise is self-defeating. Yet, as we shall see in the chapter on international trade, protectionism is just as self-defeating. All the above statements do not mean that we need patronize only domestic brands. Many Japanese products are substantially manufactured here; certainly we can patronize these brands and generate employment. If ordinary citizens and enterprise focus on our individual and collective purchasing needs, for example buying locally made products, we will always have a rich and large domestic market. This means that we won't face conditions such as what we have presently.

If reason and balance were observed by all players in the economy, we would find free trade more palatable. We certainly wouldn't find so many on welfare or extended unemployment benefits. It has not been just on Wall Street that reason and balance seemed to have been overlooked over the years, but on Main Street as well.

Detroit and the consumers with their high level of debt condition seems to indicate that they were not "well grounded." During the speculative housing bubble years, the construction industry, the financial system, and the speculators—who were too numerous to count—seemed to be living in a fantasy land. Enterprise in general was consumed by the desire to squeeze every dollar of profit out of business through unnecessary off-shoring of jobs. I suspect, today, we have more large sized homes which not enough of us, the ordinary citizens, can sensibly afford.

Because of the speculation fiasco, pension funds have to purchase higher-risk paper, hopefully to secure higher returns, to be able to meet future pension obligations. Banks have to impose higher intermediation charges to cover past losses within a reasonable period of time. Trying to print money for its low interest-rate impact is really just like pushing on a string. Too many cannot buy because they have no jobs. Those living hand to mouth can only afford to buy imported goods.

If it seems to the reader that all these moneymaking schemes seem to hark back to the days when people believed in alchemy, it does to me, too.

Now, let us examine various industries in the manufacturing sector.

Our Clean-Energy Industry

This category includes wind and solar power, biofuels, and energy efficiency. The government is presently pushing development in these areas through fiscal policy. Through the Recovery Act of 2009 and related programs, the government provided energy funding of $5.4 billion to small businesses in the clean-energy industries. These funds compliment the 2,800 loans totaling $656 million that the Small Business Administration approved for renewable energy businesses from 2006 to 2009. [34] In 2007, the Department of Commerce suggested that the size of the "green" economy is so small that we will need growth in other investments areas (and some consumer spending) to bring the economy to normal. While this is mainly true, the fact is, its emphasis will create jobs in the other sectors in the economy. The Environmental Protection Agency's

(EPA) Energy Star program will impact durable goods favorably. Smart-grid technology will reduce utility costs of power and water for the consumer. Advanced-design batteries will not only create new jobs but help reduce imports of oil. The impact created by gaining energy independence will strengthen the competitiveness of the rest of the economy.

Energy efficiency has a similar effect. The report also features a 2003 start-up company producing biodiesel and clean diesel from algae oil. Under the Recovery Act grant of $21.8 million, it will build its first integrated algae fuel refinery. There is also a Recovery Act grant for $4 million to Universal Display Corporation with the goal of establishing a pilot manufacturing line for organic light-emitting diodes, or OLEDs. [34] These developments will mean jobs and will impact the rest of the economy favorably.

It must be remembered that it was only in 2006 that we started to emphasize the greening of the economy. At that time, the green economy was considered to be too small to make a significant positive impact on employment. However, since then, significant strides in the technology and the roll-out of support programs will indeed make a difference in the total levels of employment. However, it will not be enough in the immediate future to materially reduce unemployment.

Low and steady energy prices will help in the global economic recovery, stimulating consumer spending by lowering the cost of transportation of the consumer. In our country, the lower cost of fuel could significantly improve spending on other consumer needs, and therefore enhance job creation.

Since the end of 2007, the numbers of high wage employment in the wind power industry totaled 85,000. [35] There are a number also employed in other renewables such as solar, water, biogas, and other alternative fuels. Hydrogen use from water, as fuel cells, is used in several power plants.

As more tax-credits funding becomes available, weatherization of homes and commercial buildings will mean substantial increases in employment numbers in the construction industry, as well as for suppliers. The numbers employed here will far exceed the present numbers employed in the wind power industry.

The tax credits for energy-efficient appliances, through the Energy Star program, are creating substantial increases in its demand. Patronizing domestically produced appliances, whether of foreign or domestic brands, will help improve the employment situation.

The increasing use of gas for home heating, in lieu of fuel oil, helps our domestic gas producing industry. Whatever favors the domestic producer over imports (tariffs excepted) helps generate greater employment. Of course, a big hope for substantially and significantly reducing oil consumption is in green diesel and biodiesel from algae. If the pilot manufacturing plant is found to be viable, that may be the answer to our desire to displace oil imports with locally produced clean energy.

The Department of Commerce, Economics and Statistics Administration categorizes green products and services into various types of green activities: pollution control, resource conservation, and environmental assessment.

In 2007, the green services industries absorbed nearly three-quarters of all green jobs. Manufacturing accounted for 10 to 11 percent of green jobs. Construction was only responsible for about 12 to 13 percent of employment. [36] Using the broad definition of green activity, renewable/alternative energy production accounted for 13 percent of total green activity. The broad definition includes the relatively large sectors of nuclear electricity generation services and biofuels. Energy conservation accounted for 32 percent, resource conservation accounted for 27 percent, 24 percent for pollution control and four percent for environmental assessment.

Wholesale trade, as well as administrative support and remediation services, accounted for two of the largest green industries in the services sector. In 2007, total employment in the green economy totaled 2,382,000. Shipments amounted to $516 billion. [36] The green share of the economy is relatively small. However, its impact on other industries will be substantial once the stimulus package of 2010 takes full effect.

The fast growth of productivity in the manufacturing sector has led to declines in numbers employed in energy manufacturing as well as the rest of the industries within the sector. Production processes have just become more labor efficient. However, due to the stimulus package, growth has managed to remain constant and even at a much higher level at this point and in the green services sector especially.

The agricultural sector has been producing a significant amount of biofuels like corn-based ethanol. Many people believe that ethanol is not really a very profitable or economically worthwhile policy. It drives up the price of corn which negatively impacts many food processing and industrial companies. It also is an additional burden to government, which subsidizes its production.

It would seem more economically worthwhile to scrap this program and instead import sugar-based ethanol from Brazil, which can supply it at a lower price. A more efficient and effective policy would be to import sugar-based ethanol at a price that would not need subsidy. The rationale behind this proposal is that it would stimulate Brazil's economy, which would favorably impact our exports to them, especially of agricultural equipment. This idea, of course, has to be given more thought and study as the agricultural sector at this time may not be sufficiently prosperous. But even now, a moderate loss of demand for corn may not hurt corn producers. It may be made up for by an increase in demand from the food processing and industrial products industry sectors. Because of our open economy, we have few economically inefficient industries, whether in goods producing or services. Agriculture, especially, is a highly efficient and competitive sector. It is of course important to realize that this sector requires a high volume of production and sales to remain profitable.

Our total exports of environmental products exceeded imports. Total exports amounted to $40,865,798,338 in 2008, and in the downturn year of 2009, it still amounted to $35,784,432,609. Total imports of environmental products amounted to only $14,788,307,498 in 2009. [37] It seems obvious that we need a technological advantage to be able to compete in the manufacturing sector.

Aerospace Industries

Aerospace manufacturing is one of our most competitive industries. In medium and long range commercial aircraft, there are really two major companies that dominate this area of aircraft demand, Boeing and Airbus of Western Europe. The Russian medium and long range commercial aircraft are only used by them, mainly, and some of the old members of the Soviet Union. In defense and space equipment, we also are highly competitive as is Russia, France, Sweden, and the U.K. In corporate and personal aircraft, there are a larger number of companies in this sub-sector. Competition comes mainly from Canada.

The whole sector is really either a duopoly or oligopoly, which the science and art of economics term the structure of the industries. In a duopoly, we have two companies that cater to a market. In oligopoly, on the other hand, there a few more companies dominating the market. It simply means there are so few players or companies, so that competition comes mainly in the form of quality or features of their products. This product differentiation and cost-plus pricing are almost like monopoly pricing and behavior. It is essentially not a price-determined market. Each company seeks a competitive advantage through technological advancements that enhance the safety of users as well as distance capabilities at the most efficient cost-per-passenger mile of use. The latter means the total cost of operating the aircraft to a destination divided by the number of miles flown, and then divided by the seating capacity. This is a rather secure industry, although China is seeking to develop an aerospace industry.

Total value of aerospace shipments for 2009 in current dollars amounted to $177.2 billion. Total value of U.S. aircraft and parts shipments in the same year in current dollars amounted to $152.4 billion. Total annual average employment amounted to 503,900. Value of our exports amounted to $92.5 billion, value of imports amounted to $35.8 billion. [38]

Motor Vehicle Industry

This is one of the larger industries. Total 2009 sales of new U.S. cars and light trucks numbered 10,393,000. This is a sharp decline from 16,848,000 vehicles in 2004. In the same year, American brands commanded 44.1 percent, its lowest share of the overall market. On the other hand, Japanese vehicles numbered

40.5 percent, its highest share since 2004. Total U.S. real GDP, including bodies, trailers, and parts, amounted to $155.2 billion in 2007. Total employment as of 2006 numbered 242,000. In the 12 months in 2009, exports amounted to $36.249 billion. Imports amounted to $91.246 billion of all road motor vehicles. U.S. trade flows in 2009 of medium and heavy trucks and tractors show exports at $2.585 billion, while imports amounted to $4.135 billion. We are definitely not very competitive in this industry. [39]

However, Detroit's Big Three auto and truck manufacturers have reorganized themselves and at present are displaying a highly competitive capability, which might soon render all these import and export figures slightly irrelevant. We could generate a substantial number of employments in the short and medium term if this momentum succeeds. We could generate a lot more exports and reduce imports.

Air Conditioning, Warm Air Heating, and Commercial Industrial Refrigeration Equipment

In 2005, production in these sectors was carried out by more than 800 U.S. manufacturing facilities around the country and amounted to over $35 billion. [40] This was the latest data available from the Census of Manufacturers.

Contractors install virtually all the residential and commercial central air-conditioning and refrigeration equipment in the United States. In 2006, the number of plumbing, heating, and air-conditioning contractors employed 982,500. This number has been increasing since 1970, when there were only 429,800 employees in these areas. [40]

Total employment of industry production workers of air conditioning, warm-air heating equipment, commercial industrial refrigeration equipment manufacturing, and motor vehicle air conditioning is 114,000 employees, of which 87,200 were production workers in 2006. [40]

This industry has held stable since 1970, but seems to have net import competition since the year 2000 when it had a total of 148,100 employees and 116,000 production workers. [41] Contractors in this industry, including plumbing, increased in number of employees, and have consistently increased almost every year since 1970. Since most contractors would be considered part of the service sector, it shows the growing preference of workers to learn service sector work, rather than manufacturing.

Again, this major manufacturing industry shows the contraction in number of production workers.

Metal Working Equipment/Machine Tools

This industry has over 8,000 companies producing the above products. Employees numbered over 184,000, making it a rather large producer. Its revenues amounted to $28 billion. Again, exports of $6.6 billion were less than half of U.S. imports of $13.650 billion. Increased competition from Asian imports and shifting of manufacturing to China and India, plus rising production costs, export controls, and licensing procedures are among some of the top international issues of the industry. Credit availability issues since the start of the recession is another problem facing manufacturers. As the Big Three automakers accounted for the major share of the metalworking industry, it has naturally faced a substantial fall in demand. We all know two of the Big Three went bankrupt and Ford Motor was the only one to make a major comeback recently. The industry is asking for a lower tax burden for U.S. manufacturers and increased tax-credits programs. [42]

The Printing Machinery and Equipment Industry

The industry has 427 companies and 14,000 employees. Total industry annual revenues are around $3 billion. U.S. exports of $1.137 billion were also again substantially less than U.S. imports of $1.661 billion. The top international trade issues are intellectual property, high tariff barriers, and non-tariff barriers. Foreign exchange rates are also a major issue. Again, we have high relative cost of production. Since the top six major foreign companies are based mostly in Germany, with four companies there, one in Switzerland, and one in Japan, it seems the foreign companies get concessions from their governments. After all, we have lower overall compensation than Germany and Switzerland, and just a little higher than Japan.

We certainly have to work out government policy to aid various manufacturing industries such as these in order to become more competitive with foreign markets. [43]

Agricultural Equipment Industry

This manufacturing industry is one of our most competitive. Despite our advantages, with exports totaling $9.8 billion, imports still amounted to $7.3 billion. [44]

Construction and Mining Machinery

This is another of our larger and more competitive industries. We have 1,200 companies supplying equipment parts and servicing of equipment. There is also a great deal of remanufacturing now of worn-out engines and parts. We are home to the world's largest manufacturer of construction machinery, Caterpillar, Inc., based in Peoria, Illinois. The industry has annual revenues of around $26.9 billion. Total annual exports amount to around $23.7 billion, which means the bulk of our production goes to export markets. Our annual imports total $14.8 billion, approximately. The top five international markets are Canada, Australia, China, Mexico, and Europe. The industry is asking for tax reform and lower or more stable energy costs. The forging of the steel and other metals required for construction and mining machinery requires a great deal of energy. [45]

The Food Processing and Packing Machinery Industry

This is a medium-sized industry. We have over 2,000 companies in this field, employing a total of over 30,000 people. Our annual exports amounted to around $2.063 billion. Our annual imports total around $2.931 billion. The top five foreign companies are based in Western Europe. We have some of the biggest and most well-known companies in this industry. It is the smaller players in the industry that are facing greater competition from Taiwan and now China, with cheaper equipment. Because of this, our manufacturers either produce in those countries for our domestic markets and other world markets, or produce parts for the domestically produced products. In this industry, food safety is a major issue, especially against foreign companies exporting to our domestic markets. In this industry our higher total wage costs have forced many companies to shift manufacturing to Taiwan or China in order to remain competitive. [46]

The Materials Handling Equipment Industry

This is one of our larger industries. Around 1,692 firms employ approximately 79,000 people. [47] They also generate around $30 billion. U.S annual exports totaled $6 billion while our annual imports were around $6.5 billion. We have some of the best known firms in the industry. Japan and Germany are our major competitors. Our top five international markets are Canada, Mexico, Belgium, the United Kingdom, and Brazil. The top domestic manufacturer competitiveness is unstable with high energy costs, high raw material costs, and the need for tax reform.

Some conclusions:

Industries that produce capital equipment are cyclical. Unless the product wears out or new equipment for expansion is needed, there is no need for a firm to purchase these products.

Secondly, the customers for these products used them mainly for business. Therefore the rate of return of these products must be within the range the buyer needs in order to stay in business. In more technical language, the price given for durability and productivity must at least equal the net present value of the product. Thirdly, if accelerated depreciation for tax purposes were allowed, it would certainly help the industry to sell more of their products and lower their costs of production. This is the equivalent of a tax credit, but it is more conducive to competitiveness and faster equipment replacement—even taking into consideration more product improvements.

At this time we do need tax reform that enables our vital export industries to compete more effectively. It is better to work in this direction than toward tax exemptions for industries, which enables them to earn very high rates of return. If we focus on tax reforms, which allow a measure of direct cost pricing for our major export industries (as many other exporting countries do) we can compete better. Either that or we seek to impose rules in international trade that disallow exporters from using direct cost pricing, so that our domestic and foreign markets are protected from excess competition.

Many years ago the author worked for a small welding-equipment company in Australia which used direct cost pricing to enable us to compete. This is an issue I believe is unimportant in the computer and electronics industry, where product differentiation is great. However, tax reform through accelerated depreciation would enable our firms to outsource less. In this industry, as in most engineering industries, many jobs have been outsourced to Taiwan and China.

Inflation—especially asset inflation—and instability in energy prices due to speculation and rising food prices has rendered our manufacturing industries more vulnerable to foreign competition. This is so not only in our world markets but in our own domestic markets.

We could use more government assistance in the form of research money for our traditional manufacturing industries. Research can be directed at seeking more efficient and effective manufacturing processes and machinery.

Assistance is needed for research spending because of the preponderance of small and medium-size firms in the sector. They have very little resources for research needs. The burden of government has also been increasing, and this is reflected in higher taxes and fees. This leads to an ever-rising cost of living and thus a higher cost of doing business.

The overall situation exacerbates the problem of high welfare spending, which of course translates into higher taxes. In fact, as most of us in the private sector see it, government employees have better retirement and health care benefits. While we seek optimum public services, it must be understood that these should be provided using the most efficient and effective means in order to keep the cost of living down. Otherwise, the competitiveness of our enterprise will weaken and we will lose out in our world market share for a larger and larger number of our enterprises.

We cannot allow anymore, other emerging market countries to use export led growth at the expense of our most open domestic markets. It is because we have the largest markets besides being one of the most open so that they target our markets. While they do this most of their markets are protected from our other capital equipment exports. Thus it is unfair to our workers and industries. [47]

Durable and Non-durable Consumer Goods Production Industries

Consumer goods are purchased, naturally, according to a set of values far different from those governing the purchase of capital equipment. The value of a product to the customer is based on need, taste, quality, and for its ability to enhance the quality of the consumer's life. While consumers purchase the same product, and consume more or less than others for reasons that differ for each purchaser, they fall under a common observation: consumer goods are often purchased based fundamentally on one's vision of life and of oneself. So we find excessive consumption of food, alcohol, tobacco, and even prohibited drugs as an outcome of one's inability to acquire the right vision of what life truly is about.

The ideal is an appreciation of oneself and the ability to live in a healthy way. Some may be focused on a healthy and individually expressive lifestyle while others are not (or cannot). Thus, the reasons for purchasing a product are based on an individual's state of spiritual, physical, mental, and emotional health. These faculties reflect one's degree of wisdom, self-control, and state of contentment as well as joy, happiness, and the fulfillment one feels in life. Either that or the individual carries negative stress from the lack of an adequate amount of faith, spirit of generosity, and hope. When this is the case, one experiences boredom or anxiety or a negative restlessness focused on the fulfillment of sensual preoccupations which often lead to a physically and emotionally self-destructive and corrupt manner of living life.

Some people seek to conform to the routine of working, ambition for rank and higher income, or become preoccupied with something like football or the opposite sex or eating and drinking. Few seek to live a finer life and elevate one's state and life. Few understand and seek the "road less travelled" or a more secluded life that allows one to examine one's life in meaningful terms.

Few take heed of what Socrates said: "The unexamined life is not worth living." How many appreciate the poems of Robert Frost and the paintings of present-day artist Thomas Kinkaid, which seek to give men a better appreciation of peace? To some, "less is more" for the freedom it gives one to live life in a carefully considered manner identity. It is through this process that we "bear much fruit," to quote from the New Testament.

We cannot arrive at an adequate perception as to what our true and unique identity is, unless we examine our lives by the standards taught us by the great religions, which can also help us correctly interpret spiritual laws. Only through this process can we hope to truly know ourselves, so that we may be able to live and express ourselves in an elevated and finer state of living. The art of living is nothing more than living by one's unique personality and resources and values. We seek to give of ourselves in our own unique way—one that conforms with excellence.

When we examine our lives by the light of spiritual truths and seek to live by these truths rather than by merely materialistic ones, we "die to ourselves," which is necessary to bear much fruit. As the New Testament says, "for a grain of wheat must fall to the ground and die and be reborn before it will bear much fruit."

One must always consider life as a gift from the Creator and be thankful for whatever challenges one is given. It is the challenge which tests our spiritual, intellectual, and emotional resources.

We should not rely mainly on government or enterprise to bring about changes in our inadequate incomes or economic insecurity. We must depend instead on ourselves and others to relieve us of our present stress and discomfort.

In the late 1960s and early 1970s, when I was in Australia, I saw some truly colorful clothing that seemed to enhance the masculinity of a man and, on the female side, to accentuate the beauty of the Australian woman. I could not resist purchasing some of those shirts and shoes. Home décor and modern, colorful furniture from Scandinavia was being sold in department stores in Sydney. It really was like an art, clothing one's self and creating a home environment that was uplifting to one's spirit.

Today, China exports modern showers, which enhance intimacy between husband and wife or between lovers. The designs of toilets and fittings all provide a sense of contemporary elegant living. All these can be obtained for practically a little more than the old colorless and functional shower, bath, toilet, and fittings.

Business can be a more colorful, exciting, and fulfilling endeavor than just the single-minded focus of making the most money through the lowering of costs and seeking more markets. This is really nothing more than "economic imperialism" as perceived by countries that resist our influence. Why insist on a single-minded standard business focus of making even more profits when one can gain more influence through the expression of creativity and imagination and spirit? It is my opinion that if we truly focus on the most fundamental needs of the consumer, the community, and the country, we will out-compete and outmaneuver the competition. While the individual is central to his own economic security through the acquisition of work, imagination, and interpersonal skills, enterprise can undertake a more important role than government. Economic security of the wage earner is central to the stability and vitality of the domestic markets and greatly governs the economic and political power and influence of the nation.

[27] U.S. Department of Labor, Bureau of Labor Statistics, Industries at a Glance, Forestry and Logging: NAICS

[28] Bureau of Labor Statistics, Industries at a Glance, Mining, Quarrying, and Oil Extraction: NAICS 21

[29] Bureau of Census, Survey of Current Business, Real Value Added by Industry (2005-2008), (Millions of Chained Index Dollars)

[30] Department of Labor, Bureau of Labor Statistics, Industries at a Glance, Construction: NAICS 23

[31] Bureau of Census, (Construction NAICS 23) Industry Facts (2008)

[32] National Association of Manufacturers (NAM), www.nam.org

[33] Bureau of Labor Statistics, TED: The Editor's Desk, March 30, 2009, "Manufacturing Compensation Costs in Foreign Countries and U.S., 2007"

(34) Department of Energy, EERE "How the Recovery Act Helps Small Energy Business, Plus Energy Star…"

(35) Scottrade-Quotes and Research/Scottrade Research-News and Commentary- "G.E. Wind Blade Tour Gives Americans Opportunity to Pledge Support for Clean Energy Future"

(36) U.S. Department of Commerce: Economics and Statistics Administration: "Measuring the Green Economy (2007)"

(37) U.S. Department of Commerce, International Trade Administration: Economics and Statistics Administration: "Import and Exports of Environmental Products"

(38) U.S. Department of Commerce, International Trade Administration: Key U.S. Aerospace Statistics (revised 2008)

(39) U.S. Department of Commerce, International Trade Administration: Office of Transportation and Machinery; Government and Industry Sources (2009), U.S. Motor Vehicle Industry, Domestic and International Trade Quick Facts

(40) Air conditioning, Heating, and Refrigeration Institute, Economic Statistics NAICS 333415

(41) Census of Manufacturers and Annual Survey of Manufactures, Total Employment of Industry Production Workers 2008

(42) Motor Metal Working Equipment/Tools, www.trade.gov/mas/manufacturing/00AI/metalworking_equipment_swap

(43) Printing Machinery and Equipment Industry, www.trade.gov/mas/manufacturing, DoC/ITA

(44) DoC/ITA www.trade.gov/mas/manufacturing

(45) Construction and Mining Machinery Industry, DoC/ITA
      www.trade.gov/mas/manufacturing DoC/ITA

(46) The Food and Processing Industry, DoC/ITA www.trade.
      gov/mas/manufacturing

(47) The Materials Handling Equipment Industry, DoC/ITA
      www.trade.gov/mas/manufacturing

CHAPTER 7

THE SERVICE-PROVIDING SECTOR

This sector provides the largest amount of spending in our economy. The availability and affordability of services in our economy is essential for the ease, comfort, and luxuries they provide. A life of sufficient ease and comfort is really available for all. If one wants five star dining, they are generally available almost all over the country's cities. If one is more frugally inclined perhaps he or she can perceive the luxury of enjoying a bag of french and a soda, or a cup of specially-brewed coffee along with the family–oriented ambiance of a McDonald's, or a pastry and coffee from Starbucks. We have the luxury of being able to enjoy affordable and fast-service dining at convenient locations, governed by some of the highest standards of sanitation and cleanliness that governments impose in almost all countries of the world. Here in Las Vegas, one can avail oneself of first-class rooms and amenities from casino hotels for very low prices. You can enjoy a truly fine Chinese buffet in the west side of Las Vegas for a little over $11.00 per person.

At one time in history, these standards of richness, taste, and quality of dining and accommodations were the privilege only of emperors and kings and the very affluent. Today, they are available to us, the common people. If you seek exotic, individually prepared dishes, taken with a glass of fine wine or a cold glass of a special beer, it is available at affordable prices. Perhaps we cannot afford to have these frequently, but surely we can afford it, say, once every few months.

The books produced by our publishing industries and the movies and music from our motion picture and music industries are all available at affordable prices. Broadway shows, spectator sports, museums, gaming establishments, parks, as well as beautiful, scenic outdoor environments, are available to us at affordable rates.

Most housing available provides us with adequate amounts of shelter and comfort, especially compared to most other countries in the world. Our police and fire protection services are generally governed by rules and training of high standards of conduct and equipment. While sometimes there are scandalous behaviors by the police, they are not common occurrences. In most states, the roads of the major cities are not overly congested. This is also true of our public service offices, like the post office and the motor vehicles departments. All these we get at comparatively low tax rates and prices.

Our social assistance services are among the better ones available in the world. While government and enterprise are still seeking to make health care available and affordable to all, there is no doubt in our minds and hearts that, as a rule, our health care standards are among the highest and finest available. At this point of time, over forty million Americans out of a total population of about three hundred million are without private sector health care. However, they can generally secure government-funded health care for free, otherwise known as Medicaid. It is said that in other countries like Britain and Canada, socialized medicine is available for all. It is common knowledge, however, that waiting times for a simple surgery or sometimes doctor appointments can take a while. The latest news on the Internet is that Canada is having problems funding their health care.

Convenient banking is available to virtually anyone with a good record of personal financial governance. Our mutual funds, pension funds, insurance companies, and trust companies all offer highly affordable and competitive rates for the management of our savings and investments, and financial security for our family and for our retirement years.

America has first-class community colleges, colleges, and universities, not to mention many other institutions of learning and research made more available and affordable through scholarships and government-sponsored low-cost and long-term loans. Military service gives one the right to affordably attend one of our country's schools.

Our military and defense industries, throughout our history, have provided us with a level of security virtually unequalled. Our governments have sought to provide us with openness and transparency, freedom from graft and corruption, and governing standards that only very few governments provide. All these, we get at comparatively low tax rates.

Our retail and wholesale trade industries seek to provide consumer goods, ranging from the least to the most expensive, at the highest standards of quality with the least possible trade intermediation prices. Our wholesale and retail trade industries are among the most efficient and effective providers of services for consumer goods, not to mention capital equipment.

Our waste-management and utilities give us affordable waste disposal, power, water, TV, and computer network services at highly competitive and affordable rates.

Our non-profit organizations provide highly efficient and effective relief from needs arising from adversity aside from temporary economic situations. There are shelters, meals, and counseling for the homeless. There are organizations like Feed the Hungry which seeks to provide meals for those with inadequate incomes, not only in America but also in other countries. There are organizations which cater to battered women and children, who have left their homes and are in need of temporary shelters and meals. Our museums and art galleries in New York provide, at nominal prices, some insightful and inspiring works of art, archaeological findings, and examples from natural history, comparable to any of the finest in the world.

The author is not trying to say that our present economic circumstances are beautiful, without reservation, nor acceptable to us as a people. But besides the freedoms vested in us as a people by our adherence to the constitution, there are the vast and full range of economic opportunities for freedom from hunger, lack of shelter, adequate clothing, or freedom from want of sufficient economic opportunities for exploiting our gifts and talents, values, and desired lifestyle.

If one seeks to escape the confines of a job, there are no restrictions to other available opportunities. One can turn to the arts, non-profits such as relief organizations, to sports, to the preaching of a faith, research, or to starting one's own business. There are very few countries in the world where you will find the spirit of giving back to community and country that we have here.

In whatever we offer in return of expected rewards, we have, of course, to abide by high standards of delivery of either a good or service. Opportunities are vast, but competition is also great. We live in a highly competitive world. We cannot have a high standard of living except through competition governed by the rules of fair play. Seeking protectionism will raise our cost of living, as well as the costs of doing business, which will eventually force our most efficient and effective industries to relinquish our foreign markets. Our export industries are, as a rule, the highest wage providers in our economy.

Competition demands excellence from its players, even the average players. One may not be a Michael Jordan in basketball or a Tiger Woods or an Arnold Palmer in golf nor a Buffett in investments, or a pioneer like the founders of Microsoft, Google, Oracle, and other Silicon Valley greats. Still one has the opportunity to demand and express oneself, and have a lifestyle that conforms to personal standards of excellence. The rules of excellence are governed by the personal gifts, talents, and aptitudes that we all possess, but this requires cultivation, development, and disciplined conformity to duty, to ourselves, and to others. It is not measured by the amount of money or recognition we earn. It is governed essentially by our spirit and the spirit it gives us to manifest our courage and generosity.

Look at the soldier, the dedicated family man, the selfless community or national leader. In them you will perceive what I am saying about living a life of excellence. To people with these kinds of values, opportunities are always present as well as doors that open to welcome them. Even a family man has the hearts of his family members and friends to welcome him. His personality exudes his spirit of loyalty and generosity. Whether a person is a father, mother, brother or a sister, or a friend, a wife or husband or lover, they will always find a warm heart to welcome them.

Even a business leader, who manifests more of a heart to his stakeholders, will usually be more remembered than an employer with his so-called genius. His stockholders think of his abilities to constantly produce higher returns without due concern for the other stakeholders, especially the country and the national interest. Witness the drama of 2010 between Wall Street, Washington, and the people. Witness the scorn people have for these people. Scorn may be too human a response, but it is the product of the flawed economic belief that greed is good. Such is the impact on those who do not adequately search for the basic truths or those who deny its validity.

As the scriptures say, "the wages of sin is death." (Romans 6:23) The darkness can make our lives so full of regrets and bitterness. Consequences of the darkness can be very tragic. Its victims deserve our compassion rather than our scorn, much less our hatred. Hate in our hearts should be directed at the sin rather than the sinner. It could have happened to anyone who is not made of the sterner stuff. How many of us can turn down temptations?

Now, let us turn to the economic opportunities and threats obtaining in the economy. Before I illustrate a table showing the various service industries with their real value added to total GDP, let me remind the reader of the value of exploring one's inner world and getting to know oneself, one's aptitudes, discipline, and the amount of faith one has in himself. This is to be able to fully realize and seize opportunities offered during these very difficult times. Even in this period of recession, there are industries that are either growing or resisting a major downturn in spending by consumers and businesses.

Real Value Added by Industry
[Billions of chained (2005) dollars]
Release date: May 25, 2010

Line		2004	2005	2006	2007	2008	2009
1	Gross domestic product	12,263.8	12,638.4	12,976.2	13,254.1	13,312.1	12,987.4
2	Private industries	10,713.8	11,052.5	11,385.5	11,633.4	11,619.6	11,313.9
3	Agriculture, forestry, fishing, and hunting	122.7	127.1	128.1	120.8	132.3	138.4
4	Farms	97.9	102.0	99.1	91.6	103.4	...
5	Forestry, fishing, and related activities	24.8	25.1	28.8	29.1	28.2	...
6	Mining	229.3	192.0	207.6	198.3	199.0	206.3
7	Oil and gas extraction	156.5	128.6	146.3	138.6	130.5	...
8	Mining, except oil and gas	39.1	36.3	35.2	33.3	31.7	...
9	Support activities for mining	34.2	27.2	26.8	26.5	34.5	...
10	Utilities	215.8	205.7	207.1	214.3	221.2	228.1
11	Construction	619.9	611.7	593.8	570.9	551.8	497.2
12	Manufacturing	1,517.9	1,568.0	1,636.6	1,709.8	1,647.4	1,550.6
13	Durable goods	817.7	877.6	937.5	975.8	978.4	904.7
14	Wood products	30.9	33.0	32.7	35.9	35.9	...
15	Nonmetallic mineral products	45.7	45.3	40.1	40.5	37.7	...
16	Primary metals	60.2	53.7	46.5	44.0	40.4	...
17	Fabricated metal products	119.3	120.4	126.1	131.0	126.5	...
18	Machinery	103.0	109.5	116.2	119.8	122.0	...
19	Computer and electronic products	144.8	183.3	223.8	248.7	273.2	...
20	Electrical equipment, appliances, and components	39.6	39.9	44.9	42.9	46.2	...
21	Motor vehicles, bodies and trailers, and parts	106.5	112.6	121.0	120.6	112.6	...
22	Other transportation equipment	69.4	76.0	79.3	90.4	90.8	...
23	Furniture and related products	32.5	34.3	36.1	31.8	28.6	...
24	Miscellaneous manufacturing	67.9	69.6	74.2	77.5	78.0	...
25	Nondurable goods	701.2	690.4	699.7	734.4	673.9	648.0
26	Food and beverage and tobacco products	162.4	172.1	193.1	205.1	189.5	...
27	Textile mills and textile product mills	27.0	23.5	20.4	21.3	16.4	...
28	Apparel and leather and allied products	16.0	16.0	15.7	15.2	14.7	...
29	Paper products	55.4	53.8	54.8	53.1	50.7	...
30	Printing and related support activities	38.0	37.5	36.5	37.5	37.3	...
31	Petroleum and coal products	144.1	139.3	120.9	120.9	123.4	...
32	Chemical products	193.1	182.7	201.6	218.3	183.5	...
33	Plastics and rubber products	66.3	65.6	59.1	66.6	60.5	...
34	Wholesale trade	717.8	725.3	747.5	766.5	761.9	754.2
35	Retail trade	818.8	838.8	854.2	867.7	822.6	785.7
36	Transportation and warehousing	346.8	369.7	386.1	397.7	388.0	377.1
37	Air transportation	54.9	55.7	57.5	60.3	56.2	...
38	Rail transportation	26.9	27.0	27.3	27.4	24.6	...
39	Water transportation	6.2	9.3	14.9	18.9	21.0	...
40	Truck transportation	110.2	118.9	125.3	129.6	128.4	...
41	Transit and ground passenger transportation	21.5	21.2	21.9	22.1	21.7	...
42	Pipeline transportation	10.8	10.4	9.8	11.5	11.6	...
43	Other transportation and support activities	85.1	91.9	93.8	91.3	90.1	...
44	Warehousing and storage	31.6	35.3	36.6	38.4	37.2	...
45	Information	549.5	592.6	598.3	633.9	642.6	653.0
46	Publishing industries (includes software)	141.2	151.2	131.2	143.5	142.9	...
47	Motion picture and sound recording industries	58.1	56.3	58.4	58.9	57.4	...

Real Value Added by Industry
(Billions of Chained (2005) Dollars)
Release Date: May 25, 2010

48	Broadcasting and telecommunications	273.5	311.4	326.4	357.9	365.6	...
49	Information and data processing services	77.1	73.6	82.6	74.0	77.5	...
50	**Finance, insurance, real estate, rental, and leasing**	**2,465.5**	**2,606.5**	**2,716.2**	**2,775.5**	**2,821.1**	**2,752.0**
51	**Finance and insurance**	**947.8**	**1,028.5**	**1,097.1**	**1,081.8**	**1,116.6**	**1,085.9**
52	Federal Reserve banks, credit intermediation, and related activities	434.1	470.7	466.1	472.8	456.3	...
53	Securities, commodity contracts, and investments	150.4	183.0	208.1	179.2	160.1	...
54	Insurance carriers and related activities	331.0	337.5	361.3	383.8	450.4	...
55	Funds, trusts, and other financial vehicles	32.3	37.3	41.4	47.5	56.6	...
56	**Real estate and rental and leasing**	**1,517.8**	**1,577.9**	**1,619.4**	**1,693.2**	**1,704.2**	**1,665.8**
57	Real estate	1,370.6	1,424.9	1,440.0	1,502.3	1,523.9	...
58	Rental and leasing services and lessors of intangible assets	147.1	153.1	179.5	191.1	180.4	...
59	**Professional and business services**	**1,393.1**	**1,461.8**	**1,511.0**	**1,551.3**	**1,574.6**	**1,526.9**
60	**Professional, scientific, and technical services**	**837.5**	**875.6**	**916.6**	**940.6**	**957.8**	**940.6**
61	Legal services	191.3	194.5	191.6	187.4	175.2	...
62	Computer systems design and related services	116.2	129.3	143.3	159.5	168.4	...
63	Miscellaneous professional, scientific, and technical services	530.3	551.8	581.9	594.8	616.6	...
64	**Management of companies and enterprises**	**221.1**	**217.7**	**219.8**	**216.9**	**222.0**	**216.2**
65	**Administrative and waste management services**	**335.1**	**368.5**	**374.6**	**394.5**	**395.1**	**369.5**
66	Administrative and support services	300.3	331.3	340.7	356.3	357.3	...
67	Waste management and remediation services	34.8	37.2	33.9	38.2	37.8	...
68	**Educational services, health care, and social assistance**	**937.3**	**953.4**	**985.2**	**1,005.3**	**1,037.5**	**1,051.7**
69	**Educational services**	**123.5**	**120.1**	**121.0**	**123.1**	**125.8**	**124.5**
70	**Health care and social assistance**	**813.9**	**833.3**	**864.2**	**882.3**	**911.6**	**927.6**
71	Ambulatory health care services	389.4	406.1	426.7	433.8	452.7	...
72	Hospitals and nursing and residential care facilities	354.1	354.4	363.9	372.0	380.9	...
73	Social assistance	70.5	72.8	73.7	76.5	78.3	...
74	**Arts, entertainment, recreation, accommodation, and food services**	**472.5**	**481.6**	**496.1**	**503.1**	**496.5**	**481.3**
75	**Arts, entertainment, and recreation**	**116.7**	**117.3**	**123.0**	**123.9**	**127.0**	**124.3**
76	Performing arts, spectator sports, museums, and related activities	65.2	63.8	65.7	68.0	67.6	...
77	Amusements, gambling, and recreation industries	51.5	53.5	57.3	55.9	59.5	...
78	**Accommodation and food services**	**355.8**	**364.3**	**373.1**	**379.2**	**369.5**	**357.1**
79	Accommodation	105.0	108.7	110.3	112.9	109.6	...
80	Food services and drinking places	250.7	255.6	262.8	266.4	260.0	...
81	**Other services, except government**	**317.3**	**318.5**	**318.8**	**325.9**	**325.0**	**310.3**
82	**Government**	**1,576.3**	**1,585.9**	**1,593.2**	**1,614.1**	**1,647.1**	**1,677.6**
83	**Federal**	**501.1**	**501.8**	**500.1**	**501.6**	**515.1**	**544.3**
84	General government	435.8	438.7	438.4	441.8	459.2	...
85	Government enterprises	65.2	63.1	61.7	59.9	55.9	...
86	**State and local**	**1,075.2**	**1,084.1**	**1,093.2**	**1,112.6**	**1,132.0**	**1,133.4**
87	General government	991.0	997.7	1,006.9	1,023.7	1,038.3	...
88	Government enterprises	84.2	86.4	86.4	88.8	93.9	...
89	**Not allocated by industry [1]**	**-43.2**	**0.0**	**-12.1**	**-17.6**	**12.2**	...
90	**Addenda:**						
91	Private goods-producing industries [2]	2,481.7	2,498.8	2,565.3	2,593.3	2,528.4	2,394.0
92	Private services-producing industries [3]	8,233.2	8,553.7	8,820.1	9,040.3	9,092.0	8,919.6
93	Information-communications-technology-producing industries [4]	478.5	537.4	579.2	623.1	656.6	656.1

1. Chained (2005) dollar series are calculated as the product of the chain-type quantity index and the 2005 current-dollar value of the corresponding series, divided by 100. Because the formula for the chain-type quantity indexes uses weights of more than one period, the corresponding chained-dollar estimates are usually not additive. The value of the "Not allocated by industry" line reflects the difference between the first line and the sum of the most detailed lines, as well as the differences in source data used to estimate GDP by industry and the expenditures measure of real GDP.

2. Consists of agriculture, forestry, fishing, and hunting; mining; construction; and manufacturing.

3. Consists of utilities; wholesale trade; retail trade; transportation and warehousing; information; finance, insurance, real estate, rental, and leasing; professional and business services; educational services, health care, and social assistance; arts, entertainment, recreation, accommodation, and food services; and other services, except government.

4. Consists of computer and electronic products; publishing industries (includes software); information and data processing services; and computer systems design and related services.

Gross-Domestic-Product-by-Industry Accounts Help
Gross-Domestic-Product-by-Industry Press Release
Guide to the Interactive GDP by Industry Accounts Tables
E-mail us your questions and comments

Real Value Added by Industry
(Billions of Chained (2005) Dollars)
Release Date: May 25, 2010

It is my opinion that there is a lack of balance between the goods-producing sector and agriculture relative to the service-providing sector. In other words, we need a larger proportion of the former relative to overall GDP. Otherwise, it could mean either permanent higher levels of unemployment or over-crowding in the number of service industries, such as maintenance of either capital equipment or consumer durable goods, plumbing, restaurants, etc. This would lead to lower incomes of workers in the fields.

The total contribution of real value-added as of 2008 of the private services-producing sector amounted to $8.092 trillion. Of this, as you will see in Table 4, the largest proportion of total sector GDP are the wholesale, retail, and transportation and warehousing industries, which are dependent on either the goods-producing sector products or its imports. Also, finance, insurance, real estate, rental, and leasing industries contributed the largest share to GDP. Most of the jobs in these fields involved commission-based sales work. These jobs could become either overcrowded or their average incomes will fall.

Included in the private services-producing industries are utilities. There is at present a desire in some sectors of the economy to displace oil imports with renewable sources of energy. Thus, we are slowly changing from the use of oil to the production of power through solar and wind sources. This means a displacement of a good with a service, which is solar and wind. This is a positive development, because it helps stabilize the cost of energy, which would reduce economic volatility and the jobs that go with it.

Oil has been a basic part of our economy since we first discovered it. Its price is continually fluctuating so that it impacts consumer cost of living and the cost of doing business. The price of oil is governed only by short-term demand and supply. It can also be highly influenced by speculation in the commodities markets. These aggravate the volatility of its price. This is one of its major "diseconomies" as it is termed in economics. These diseconomies or costs to us are not reflected in the price of oil. It certainly does not reflect the long-run loss of competitiveness that it can bring to the economy. There are a lot of countries, like China and other emerging markets that subsidize their domestic price of oil. We do not. All we do to reduce oil is stockpile and release in the market as needed. But really, our policy does not do much to stabilize the price of oil.

Another major diseconomy of oil is that it is mainly available in the Middle East. This area is very unstable and our having to seek to stabilize it and also defend Israel has created a high cost of security for us. Other diseconomies are climate change, the influence of oil pollution and, of course, its effect on the health of the population.

For the above reasons, it has been worth our while to subsidize the price to buyers of renewable energy.

Table 4 and Table 5 are the latest Annual Industry Accounts for GDP. In Table 5, it is shown that a lower GDP growth in 2008 reflected downturns in fifteen of twenty-two major industry groups. The growth industries were in the professional, scientific and technical services, health care and social assistance, and government.

Wholesale Trade Subsector:

Most wholesale firms were involved either in processed agricultural and seafood and dairy and livestock products or raw farm product materials. Others were in chemicals, plastics, petroleum, beer, wine and distilled alcoholic beverages, farm supplies, books and periodicals, flowers, nursery stock and florist supplies, tobacco, and other miscellaneous non-durable goods. Lastly, the larger group was automobiles, other motor vehicles, and motor vehicle supplies or parts.

The very large firms with 10,000 or more employees are those like Costco, Sam's Club, Best Buy, etc. [50]

The Retail Trade

This is the largest employer among all the subsectors in the services sector, with a total workforce of 14,433,710. Establishments totaled 1,039,467 in the fourth quarter of 2009. The largest employers were motor vehicles and parts dealers, building materials, garden equipment and supplies dealers, food and beverage, health and personal care, clothing accessories, and general merchandise. They all had numbers of total employed from a little over one million to more than 2.8 million. Retailers of products with total work forces under a million were furniture and home furnishing, electronics and appliances, gasoline stations, sporting goods, hobby, book and music stores, miscellaneous retailers, and non-store retailers. [51]

Total workforce of firms with less than 500 employees totaled 6,314,262. Firms with 10,000 or more employees numbered only 333 but its total workforce totaled 7,635,918 in the fourth quarter of 2008.

The rank and file in retail outlets for non-durables was paid lower than for the retail outfits for durable goods. The durable-goods retailers generally paid commissions along with a slightly above-minimum wage, as basic pay. Some clothing and clothing accessories stores, sporting goods, hobby, book and music stores and pharmacies paid above minimum wage levels. Food and beverage stores, gasoline stations, and general merchandise stores generally paid just slightly above the minimum wage. Earnings of salespeople in motor vehicles and parts, furniture and home furnishings, and electronic and appliance stores were generally at median income levels. The rest, other than pharmacists, were below the median income levels.

Most non-durable goods retail is resistant to economic downturns, unlike the durable goods sales, which can be volatile. Credit availability is also a crucial economic factor for the non-durable retail trade. If large numbers of wage earners are inclined to spend their incomes totally, then even the non-durable retail trade will depend on the availability of credit.

Building material and garden equipment and supplies dealers, as a rule, are cyclical businesses dependent on the rate of construction activity in the economy. Construction activity is also somewhat dependent on the availability of credit and the standards they impose, plus overall economic activity.

High levels of retail trade activity may not necessarily translate into substantial GDP growth if most purchases are of heavy import content or even totally imported. The retail trade for consumer goods items is mostly imported, although it will substantially impact favorably on transportation and housing.

Durable consumer goods have much more domestic content and impact our factories better.

Building materials and supplies are imported in a substantial range of items, especially for hardware. However, due to the numbers employed in the retail trade, plus construction, this is a highly significant economic sector. There is some concentration in this area of the retail trade, given that it only has around 6,965 home center establishments but with 578,215 out of 1,167,637 paid employees out of a total numbers in the trade. Hardware stores had 16.349 establishments with only a total number of paid employees of 143,075.

In food and beverage retail, there appears to be a concentration in the sub-sector with fewer firms operating supermarkets and other groceries (except convenience stores). However, there seems to be more than adequate price and brand competition.

In health and personal care stores, there appears to be some concentration in the pharmacist drugstore subsector with fewer establishments of 42,129 with a total work force of 821,690. However, it also seems that there is more than adequate price and brand competition.

There does not seem to be much concentration in the gasoline station sub-sector, although in Las Vegas, this seems to be so. However, we do not seem to suffer from a lack of price and brand choices.

In the hobby, game, and toy stores sub-sectors, there appears to be some concentration of business in the hands of fewer competitors. There were only 9,287 establishments with a total workforce of 135,701.

Among department stores, there is definitely some concentration. There are only 8,553 establishments with a total workforce of 1,229,489. Warehouse clubs and supercenters are also concentrated in fewer firms. They had 4,991 establishments with a total number of 1,244,250 employees.

Pets and pet supplies stores also reflected some concentration with only 8,721 firms with a total number of employees of 101,388.

Jobs in the non-durable trade sector can be either permanent or seasonal. However, these offer rather low wage levels and there is a great deal of employee turnover. A lifetime career may be worthwhile for a relatively small number who have potential for promotion to supervisory and managerial jobs. The whole sector is dependent on total consumer spending so that it is seen as an indicator of rising or falling total economic activity.

Transport and Warehousing Service Industry

The contribution of real value added by this industry to total GDP in 2008 was $350.9 billion. [29] Real value added was based on calendar year (CY) 2000 constant dollars.

Firms employing less than 500 people numbered 169,807 with a total workforce of 1,629,628. Firms employing 10,000 or more workers number 370 but employed a total of 1,711,171 workers. This data reflects some concentration of activity among fewer competitors. Industry concentration is in air transportation, water transport, and couriers and messengers, as well as warehousing and storage. [52]

Truck transportation employed the largest workforce of 1,478,343 workers in the industry. Warehousing and storage had the second largest workforce of 709,331. Third, there were support activities for transportation with 627,327.

Wages and salaries for pilots and truck and bus drivers are higher than what obtains in, for example, the leisure and hospitality industry or retail trade. The transport jobs, however, are as a rule more stressful. While the largest workforces in the industry were in road and air transport, we also had all kinds of water transport firms. Both freight and passenger services are available and highly developed for any of the means of transport, which are road, rail, air, and water.

The government is, at present, investing substantial sums for roads, railways, and highways which would lower the cost of transport through greater efficiency. The transportation industry is a vital contributor to the competitiveness of American enterprise. The more efficient it becomes, the more competitive our economy becomes. While the transport sector contributes less than four percent real value added to total GDP, it is a major user of fuel. If fuel prices rise substantially, it could create losses for transport firms. High fuel prices would also raise transport costs, which are a major part of consumer and capital goods and service prices.

We have one of the world's most comprehensive and efficient transportation and warehousing sub-sectors. However, unlike China and some other countries, we do not have subsidized fuel. Since transport costs relative to goods and services prices are significant, our economy is in a most disadvantageous competitive situation in world trade. This is as much an issue in world trade, especially with China, as currency valuation or direct export subsidies.

Information Industry

This industry has 141,034 establishments with over 3,428,262 employees. The publishing and motion picture and sound industries are significant exporters and provide a positive contribution to our balance of trade outcome. The telecommunication sub-sector employs 1,242,078 and earns substantial revenues from

overseas calls. While the publishing industry has only 1,027,388 employees, its annual
payroll is higher than that of the telecommunications industry. The motion picture and
sound recording industries, broadcasting,
data processing, hosting and related services
and other information services employ over
1,100,000 workers with annual payroll exceed-
ing $72 billion. The combined payroll of the
publishing industries and telecommunications
exceeds $150 billion. [53]

This industry offers one of the highest average hourly earnings in the economy.

The newspaper, periodicals, book, direc-
tory, and mailing lists publishers are the major
players in the printed-paper industry. Software
publishers are major players in the publishing
field with a total workforce of 359,769, and an
annual payroll of approximately $43.6 billion.
The table reveals that the wage levels in the
software/publishing industry are among the
highest in the whole of the services sector.

The motion picture and video industries
also pay above-average wages; however, the

sound recording industries pay significantly more. Motion picture and video distribution, as well as exhibition, are significant employers but offer low average wages.

Most newspaper and periodicals publishers are finding their advertising and subscriptions being rapidly displaced by Internet-based media, which transmit news faster. Motion picture and video and sound recording industries are finding intellectual property piracy to be a significant problem. Software publishers in the U.S. are leaders but facing stiff competition from other countries. Television broadcasting is grappling with escalating costs of production. Data processing is slowly being outsourced overseas to take advantage of lower wages there. Internet publishing and broadcasting and web search portals are doing very well and have high rates of growth. Libraries and archives are being reduced in numbers as local governments seek to cut costs to counter the economic slowdown. Radio broadcasting seems to be doing well and growing steadily.

Real value added to total GDP by the information industry amounted to $653 billion. [48]

This is nearly six percent of total real value of GDP in CY 2000 GDP of $11.852 trillion. ICT (information, communications and telecommunications) industries remained strong in 2008 in spite of the economic slowdown in this same year. The industry recorded a 9 percent growth rate in the year, and accounted for 30 percent of real GDP growth in 2008. [29] The Information Industry is vital in this age of globalization.

Finance and Insurance

This industry had a real value added in CY 2008 that amounted to $1,085 billion. [48] It suffered a nearly $30 billion industry contraction in this year due to the overall economic slowdown, although overall, real GDP only experienced slower growth.

In 2008, the industry employed 6,562,546 people. Credit intermediation and related institutions such as commercial and savings banks, credit unions, and other credit intermediation firms, accounted for 3,203,232 employees. Securities, commodity contract, and investment firms employed 930,838 people. Insurance carriers and related activities employed a workforce numbering 2,409,413. [54]

All these numbers show the importance of this industry's total workforce and its purchasing power relative to other sectors and the overall economy.

Credit card issuing institutions accounted for a workforce of only 73,685. However, its industry's impact on consumption can be very significant for the durable and non-durable retail trade. Sales financing activities employed only 128,291 people, but are highly important for financial needs of small and medium-size firms.

The financial industry has, of late, been facing substantial criticism and new regulations due to its recent massive failure. It is rather difficult to find job security for most executives in this industry.

The insurance industry, except for the sales force employed on a strictly commission basis, offers more job security and industry stability. It has, however, felt the slowdown since 2008.

Pension funds require very perceptive and analytical minds for its mainly investment activities.

We have some of the most competitive financial firms in the world. It is just that sometimes their imagination where making money is concerned may be out of touch with reality. Failure of imagination is the main reason for recurring failures in the industry. This field is full of opportunities for those of sound judgment and perception.

Real Estate, Rental, and Leasing

This industry has a smaller share of our economy relative to employment numbers. Its importance is in its impact of new home sales. The industry also provides liquidity for the assets that so many in the population own.

Total number of employees in the industry was 2,309,725, of which the sales brokering part made up 1,611,159. [54] Rental and leasing services had 666,317 employees. This latter service will increase in share of numbers employed in the industry due to this recession. It will take some time before the mortgage lenders will significantly loosen their lending terms. It may take another five to six years before we return to substantially lower down payments with corresponding low interest rates. For these reasons and because of the number of foreclosures, rental and leasing services for homes will be a growing subsector of real estate.

Lessors of apartment buildings have a significant number of employees, as are lessors of non-residential buildings (except mini-warehouses).

Real estate brokers and agents number fewer than property managers of residential and non-residential property. Real estate appraisers are a small part of the industry, but usually command at least medium or average incomes.

The industry is one of the most badly hit by the recession. The numbers employed since the 2007 census have been reduced significantly. However, residential property management might provide a brighter spot as greater numbers of the population rent their homes.

Non-financial asset lessors, like video tape and disc rental, also employ a significant number. The recession favors this industry as families seek more home-based entertainment. Machinery and equipment rental and leasing will be more negatively affected by this recession as many small businesses fail. The construction industry, which is a major lessor of equipment, is one of the worst affected by this recession.

Professional, Scientific and Technical Services

In 2008, this industry provided over half the growth in real GDP. [29] Based on the 2007 economic census, the industry had 8,079,319 employees. The industry commanded reasonably higher salaries with a total annual payroll of $511.8 billion. [55]

The legal services profession, as well as accounting, tax preparation, and payroll services account for a little over 30 percent of total numbers employed by the industry.

Architectural, engineering, and related services account for around 18 percent of total industry employed. Computer systems design and related services account for about 16 percent. Management, scientific, and technical consultancy services account for a little over nine percent. Scientific research and development services had 650,804 employed. Advertising, public relations, and related services numbered a little over five percent of total. Other professional, scientific and technical services contributed around seven percent for a total of 586,882 employed. These latter services are in areas of marketing research and public opinion polling, photographic services, translation and interpretation services, and veterinary services.

Management of Companies and Enterprises

This industry employs a total of 2,779,453 people. The majority are in corporate, subsidiary, and regional managing offices. They comprised 2,626,722 in 2007 of total employed in the industry. [55] Offices of bank holding companies and of other holding companies comprised only a little more than 150,000 of the total. The numbers employed in this function are more stable even though there have been a number of failures in both Wall and Main Streets. These include high-paying jobs accompanied by substantial bonuses for good performance. There has been some decline in total earnings of this industry, mainly due to mergers and acquisitions and some managerial restructuring.

Office Administrative Services

Office administration employed over 10,195,685 workers, of which administrative and support and services accounted for 9,828,905. Office administrative services only comprised 389,567 workers. [55]

The majority of the industry's workforce was in employment services comprising 5,228,975 workers. Most of these were in temporary help services and professional employer organizations. Business support services employed 855,578 for such functions as document preparation, telephone call centers, telemarketing bureaus and other contact centers, collection agencies, credit bureaus, and other business support services.

Travel agencies and other travel arrangement services had a significant 262,023 employees. This is basically a lower-wage function or industry and its contribution of real value added was $335 billion in 2008.

Many of these jobs have been outsourced since then, and there is a continuing trend in this direction. Inflation over the past 20 years has been such that the financial marketplace demands for high rates of return have forced firms to send many of these jobs overseas.

Educational Services

This industry contributed $92.9 billion of real value added in CY 2007. It also employed a total of 565,512 people. As a whole, educational services wages are above mean wages obtaining in the economy. Only 49,201 establishments employing 426,028 workers are subject to federal income tax. There were 11,706 establishments employing 139,484 workers exempt from federal income tax. [56] These were mostly business schools, computer and management training, business and secretarial schools, professional and management development training and technical schools, as well as fine arts and sports and recreation instruction and language.

Private sector schools are vital for the training and education of high school graduates and members of the workforce seeking to learn new skills and knowledge. They are important for the supply of services that enable the workforce to gain job type mobility. This industry is usually very profitable. It has been growing at around 0.03% contribution to real value added in CY 2008. [29]

Healthcare and Social Assistance

This whole industry contributed $797.9 billion of real value added in 2008. [49]It also contributed to growth in real gross domestic product of nearly 30 percent in 2008, its largest share since 1970.

Ambulatory health care services such as physicians, mental health specialists, dentists, chiropractors, and optometrists employed a total workforce of 5,733,570. Hospitals numbered 6,529 establishments and employed a total of 5,544,361 in 2008. [56]

Nursing and residential care facilities comprised 75,730 establishments with a total workforce of 3,083,116. Social assistance had 152,391 establishments and employed 2,468,614 people.

This industry is one of our most important of the services sector, if not the most important for the physical, mental, and emotional health of our population. One of the main problems facing the economy is the high cost of health care.

There seems to be a concentration (or a shortage) of adequate competition in the medical insurance industry. There are only 178 firms with a workforce of 3,091,410. Sixty-seven firms employed 10,000 or more. There were sufficient numbers of firms with 500 to 999 employees with a total workforce of 1,143,742. There were also sufficient numbers of firms with larger workforces. The data is unclear where there is a lack of competition.

Arts, Entertainment, and Recreation

The performing arts, spectator sports, and related industries had 43,791 firms in 2007, with a total number of 441,998 employees. They were about evenly divided in numbers employed among performing arts companies, spectator sports, and promoters of performing arts, sports, and similar events. Museums, historical sites, and similar institutions numbered 7,120 with an employees workforce of 130,082. [57]

Amusements, gambling, and recreation industries had a large workforce of 1,506,120. These types of firms were golf courses, skiing facilities, fitness and recreational sports centers, bowling alleys, amusement arcades, casinos, etc. Most of these were subject to federal income tax, with some exceptions. As can be seen, this is a fairly large sector and generates high incomes for various sportsmen as well as artists. Some areas of this sub-sector provide some job security. It contributed $106.3 billion of real value added to GDP in 2008. This industry still experienced small growth in 2008. However, it is still subject to downturns in the economy.

Accommodation and Food Services

This is the largest sector within the services sector of the economy. It had a total of over 11,580,000 employees as per the Economic

2007 Census. It had over 62,746 establishments in accommodation and 566,020 in food services and drinking places. [57]

This sector is one of the more negatively affected by a downturn, especially if it is due to a large number of consumers being more frugal with their spending.

Other Services (except Public Administration)

This industry had a real value added of $236.0 billion in 2008. [29] Repair maintenance accounted for 1,286,347 employees. Personal care and laundry had 1,330,407 employees. Religious, grant-making, civic, professional, and similar organizations employed a total of 882,004. [58]

This industry is a relatively stable employer although personal care services like beauty salons and nail care may suffer in times of more frugal spending.

Conclusion: Services Sector

This sector is more likely to suffer a decrease in real incomes due to inflationary pressures. It will also be more likely to have a fall in employment levels. This rise in the unemployment rate for most of the industries in this sector will be due to more frugal spending by consumers.

The outsourcing of substantial numbers of office jobs including software, research and development, call centers, and business process outsourcing has added to the permanent loss of jobs for office employees. Unless most of these jobs are brought back into the U.S. it is my opinion that the unemployment rate will remain high for some time. It is most unlikely that the new jobs from renewable and energy-efficiency industry growth will translate into substantial offices and other services jobs.

The manufacturing sector can only make inroads into world markets and better defend itself against imports if the dollar depreciates. It has suffered substantial reduction in employment levels due to major productivity increases. Thus, it is most likely to have a sufficient impact on consumer service-sector spending. The services sector will have to rely more on the information, health care, and professional, scientific, and technical sub-sectors for growth.

However, health care may grow but its present levels are already so high as to negatively impact the competitiveness of various export industries. It also creates inflationary pressures which will negatively affect the service sector. The service sector has, as a rule, more competition and sensitivity to disposable incomes than the goods-producing sector. This will mean a decrease in real incomes for its workers.

If we could have less of an outflow of American tourists and more domestic tourism, plus the ability to attract more foreign tourists, we could create substantial employment improvements. The tourism industry is labor intensive and could also create more retail sales and the jobs that go with it.

[48] Table 4 BEA/Industry Economic Accounts, Real Value Added by Industry, Billions of Chained (2005) Dollars, Release date May 25, 2010

[49] Table 5 BEA/Industry Economic Accounts, Contributions to Percent Changes in Real Gross Domestic Product by Industry, Release date May 25, 2010

[50] The Wholesale Trade NAICS 42 DEA/Industry Economic Accounts, Industries at a Glance

[51] The Retail Trade NAICS 44-45 DEA/Industry Economic Accounts, Industries at a Glance

(52)   BEA/Transport and Warehousing, Industries at a Glance NAICS 42

(53)   BEA/Information Industry, NAICS 54, 55, 56

(54)   BEA/Financial Activities, Finance and Insurance (NAICS 52), Real Estate and Rental (NAICS 53)

(55)   BEA/Professional and Business Services/Professional, Scientific, and Technical Services/Management Companies and Enterprises /Administrative, Support, Waste Management, and Remediation Services Industries

(56)   BEA/Educational Services NAICS 61, Healthcare and Social Assistance NAICS 62

(57)   BEA/Leisure and Hospitality Services, Arts and Entertainment NAICS 71, Accommodation and Food Services NAICS 72

(58)   BEA/Other Services (except Public Administration), Repairs and Maintenance NAICS 811. Personal and Laundry Services NAICS 812, Religions, Grant making, Civic, Professional, and similar organizations NAICS 813

CHAPTER 8

INTERNATIONAL TRADE AND FOREIGN POLICY

The rationale behind international trade comes from the theory of comparative advantage, which was first proposed by a British classical economist named David Ricardo.

The theory advises exporting one's products that employ resources more productively to a country which is less productive, and importing from that country its products which employ resources more productively. To better illustrate, if some of our manufactured products and technology have greater productivity levels than, say, China's products, we seek to export to them. We, in turn, import from

China products in which they have a comparative advantage. This comparative advantage of China may come from its abundant cheap labor. Our comparative advantage stems from our technological capabilities, and our disadvantage is the relative shortage of cheap labor.

Under these circumstances, it is advisable for America to pursue a more technological and capital-intensive goods and services industries growth policy and to seek to trade with China with its abundance of cheap labor. China, on the other hand, would be advised to first seek to deploy capital and managerial talents towards goods and services industries that are labor intensive.

This vision of some economists and their theories, like the Theory of Comparative Advantage, is founded on their aspirations of prosperity and economic justice for all. Their vision and aspirations are for all men, regardless of race, color, or creed. They have absolutely no intention of favoring one over another with their principles and theories.

Different economies and peoples have different strengths and weaknesses. They have abundance in some economic resources, and a lack in other resources. The pursuit of growth and development cannot be a copy of another country's path. This is because each country faces its own strengths and weaknesses, and also, therefore, different opportunities and threats. To illustrate, Japan has a comparative advantage in engineering-based manufacturing that is highly productive. However, it suffers from a severe shortage of young workers for the lower productivity work required mainly in assembly and packaging. It also lacks sufficient numbers of caregivers consistent with the needs of its aging population.

Japan's greatest asset is its highly disciplined people, with an elite class that is very conscious of their responsibilities to provide prosperity and economic justice for all. The work environment is highly democratic, with management seeking opinions and contributions from the workers of quality and productivity enhancing ideas. They have contributed managerial ideas and principles to America and to the rest of the world that include just-in-time inventory, quality circles, etc., that bring greater prosperity for all.

Our ideals and the way we use them in policies and actions is one of political, economic, and social justice for all men and women regardless of race, color, or creed. It is my belief that this is President Obama's vision through the exercise of "soft power."

It is understood that President Obama is seeking to manifest the ideals and spirit of the American people. Those who seek to discover the spirit and ideals of the American people will perceive that it is unity and solidarity which is ultimately sought for in spite of differences in political opinions on what policies should govern the nation. This "salad bowl" is the result of peoples from all over seeking to pursue the American Dream.

The American Dream, in reality, is the desire to make a successful contribution to the world that is consonant with high ideals. These high ideals are the manifestation of faith, courage, hope, and generosity toward all.

One of our greatest leaders, President Lincoln, said in the aftermath of the Civil War, "with malice towards none, and charity for all...let us bind the nation's wounds." [59] If anyone would like to see that in international affairs, it can be perceived through our people's response and their sacrifices toward peoples in other lands who suffer in times of great tragedy and calamity.

The American people do not all speak the same language or dress the same way, nor are they always in agreement. However, they essentially agree that the people should be heard. But the common vision which weaves the spirit of unity and solidarity are their ideals and principles by which they seek to live as a people.

If any government or economic policy is inconsistent with these ideals and principles, the result will be dissension.

Diplomacy seeks to minimize conflicts and misunderstanding in foreign affairs. It is the cheapest and most effective way for countries to address their national security concerns. The less the world has to spend on military conflicts, the greater the level of security everyone attains. There is no truth these days to the idea that war creates prosperity in its aftermath. It may be true, for arms merchants, that war enables them to make more money. However, in reality, the level of prosperity and security in the world has been reduced.

What I have been trying to point out is that, contrary to the widespread belief that American society is materialistic, the truth is that the American spirit is both outward-looking and concerned with its own national interest. It is not money that is central in American life; it is security, freedom, and justice in the political, economic, and social landscape of our country and the rest of the world.

Let us now look at the current economic and trade situation and related issues so that understanding and mutual prosperity with our trading partners may be realized. The chart below reflects the financial results from U.S. international trade in goods and services.

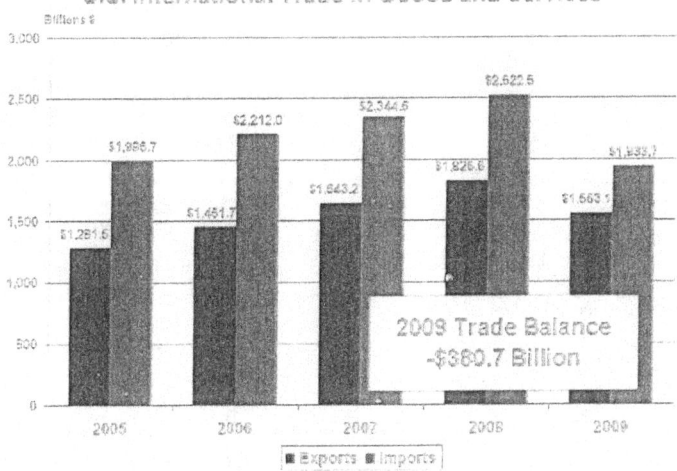

U.S. International Trade
In Goods and Services

The chart above shows an untenable trade deficit, given its duration and large amounts. [60]

The succeeding table reflects trade positions with our top 15 trading partners. [6

Total Trade (Goods)

Rank	Country	Exports (Year-to-Date)	Imports (Year-to-Date)	Total Trade (Year-to-Date)	Percent of Total Trade
---	Total, All Countries	611.7	905.5	1,517.2	100.0%
---	Total, Top 15 Countries	428.6	659.8	1,088.4	71.7%
1	Canada	122.4	138.8	261.2	17.2%
2	China	41.2	160.7	201.9	13.3%
3	Mexico	77.3	110.4	187.6	12.4%
4	Japan	29.2	55.9	85.1	5.6%
5	Federal Republic of Germany	23.2	38.3	61.5	4.1%
6	United Kingdom	24.3	23.8	48.1	3.2%
7	Korea, South	19.2	22.3	41.6	2.7%
8	France	13.0	18.6	31.6	2.1%
9	Taiwan	12.1	16.4	28.5	1.9%
10	Brazil	16.4	11.4	27.8	1.8%
11	Netherlands	16.2	9.1	25.3	1.7%
12	India	9.2	14.4	23.6	1.6%
13	Singapore	14.2	8.0	22.3	1.5%
14	Venezuela	4.9	16.4	21.3	1.4%
15	Saudi Arabia	5.8	15.3	21.1	1.4%

Total Trade

Exports

Imports

Our top five trading partners make up approximately 50 percent of our total trade. These five trading partners are Canada, China, Mexico, Japan, and Germany. With these, we suffered significant trade deficits, especially with China. Out of the 15 trading partners listed on the table above, we had only significant trade surpluses with the Netherlands,

Brazil, and Singapore. With all the others, the United Kingdom excepted, we had significant trade deficits.

Oil is a very large portion of total imports, amounting to nearly 50 percent. In order to counter this, we have to seek to be energy-import independent. Also, we have to find ways to bring down our high building and home energy costs through energy efficiency and alternative energy.

As for our non-oil imports, it is suggested that we export more automobile parts and engines to less-developed countries to support their truck and car assembly plants. They can also engage in the fabrication of pickup truck bodies. We can export to them engines and other more complex parts. It is important for us to turn the tide in the auto and truck trade game, so we strike a more balanced total trade figure.

With countries with which we have no deficit or surplus, like India, we should try to relax export of more advanced technologies.

Only by changing our trading strategy is it possible to alter the world trading order.

I lived most of my life in a Third World country before migrating to America. That is how I became familiar with so many of economic and trade issues there. Foreign exchange shortages, dollar salting, and devaluation of currency affected import prices significantly. There has been some relief from these problems when many of their workers we able either to migrate or to get jobs as overseas foreign workers (OFWs). These migrant OFWs remit substantial sums of hard currency (foreign earnings) to their families from wage earnings. Before the migration wave from mostly third to first world countries hard currency was in very much short supply in the third world. This used to cause so much instability in their economies, given their substantial reliance on imports. Many of the consumer and industrial goods which they needed were frequently in short supply.

Before the collapse of the Soviet Union and communism, America did much less of importing and exporting as it does now. However technological advances and increasing prosperity in first world countries brought a demand for more imports from the third world. This led to more world trade and the onset of globalization. Our small companies that export can use more help from our trade or commerce department. They usually need assistance for foreign trade exhibits and other promotions which they cannot quite afford. They also need information on the opportunities available in various world markets. Government budget constraints lately have been reduced thus negatively impacting the needed assistance. However, our government foreign trade offices located all over the world assist greatly these small firms by trade partners. They essentially help them diversify their markets. These small firms are usually more labor intensive than the large exporters.

The government, in its efforts for more exports of renewable energy equipment, has been allocating funds for research and development. We are competing for world leadership in this arena of trade. Renewable energy firms are small but capital intensive. Our government at present, through its trade news, is encouraging small firms to intensify their marketing efforts and diversify their export markets.

With the substantial fall in our housing and oil prices, our real incomes have risen substantially. This is so as housing and transport command a very large portion of our household budgets. The final result gives less upward wage pressures in the face of some rising prices for our imported consumer goods. These price rises are due to the depreciation of our currency. This depreciation vis-à-vis the currencies of our import partners means higher prices for our imports. The fall in the value of the dollar vis-à-vis other countries means we need more dollars to purchase the same amount of goods in their currency. We may even find some small increases in prices of our capital equipment imports from the E.U. and Japan. The net fall in our cost of living means greater competitiveness of our labor force against much cheaper labor in China and other developing countries. We are also now more competitive with other first world countries in our domestic export markets.

Through the above strategy, we can avoid the destabilizing impact of the reality of the accelerator theory in the capital goods sector, upon which the bulk of our manufacturing is focused. The accelerator theory explanation can be found in any freshman textbook in economics. Capital goods manufacturing is a very volatile sector of the economy. Orders tend to accelerate during rising levels of prosperity, and can abruptly fall with the completion of all the orders.

It has been suggested that protectionism, or the use of tariffs, is not a very good idea. However, it should be pointed out that completely free trade requires a level playing field. Rules have to be in place before any major concessions to one's domestic market are made. Otherwise, you have the case where China dominates light manufacturing and even other heavy industries while refusing to let its currency appreciate.

You have also the case of the United States economically weakened by almost continuous war since World War II, and especially by the very long Cold War.

The country has also wasted hundreds of billions amounting to nearly $2 trillion in various real estate speculative episodes since the 1970s.

There have been billions spent on stock market speculative bubble episodes which, of course, went bust. The loose lending policies of the Fed over a prolonged period of time in the 1980s, plus huge budget deficits, have caused both asset and consumer price inflation. The effect of all these is to render our country unable to adequately compete in industries other than high-tech ones. Thus, we have one of the longest recessions ever experienced. Our unemployment levels are high. No answer seems in sight to all these problems.

Many countries around the world have found their light manufacturing in labor-intensive industries decimated by competition from China. For this reason alone, they have unacceptable levels of unemployment.

The social landscape in just about every country in the world is such that to expect people to shift from cheap labor jobs to more tech-oriented jobs is not just possible.

In most emerging market countries, wages may be low but they cannot compete against China and so have high levels of unemployment and low growth. They spend more for imports due to lack of import substitution industries such as garments industries. The reason why so many emerging market countries cannot compete against China is because of a history of graft and corruption in their countries. They also engaged in many grandiose "capital intensive industries" encouraged by World Bank loans. These industries, aside from equally grandiose infrastructure investments, could not be repaid without much hardship to the population. They caused so much inflation in those countries as well as budget deficits caused by having to repay those loans.

Go to South and Central America and parts of Southeast Asia as well as Africa, and you find countries with governments buried in debts and having to constantly impose more taxes on their people. Since imposing taxes on business would be a more politically and economically suicidal approach, it is consumers who bear the greater tax burdens.

There are so many labor-intensive industries which can grow in emerging market
countries with minimal machinery requirements, for example garments and shoe manufacturing industries. These are suitable for the
cultural, social, and economic situation which
the masses in these countries possess. If a tariff
policy is chosen, then a selective rather than a
general tariff is suggested.

America, it is suggested, should consider
the use of selective tariffs. This is suggested
in many labor-intensive industry imports. For
industries like overseas call centers, as well as
business processing service imports, we should
use tariffs. Imports of high-tech service industries such as computer consulting and software
manufacture should have tariffs. There will
always be people who can do these and even
some medium manufacturing jobs such as
automobile parts, cheaper than we can here.
This is because we have always believed that
justice is the cornerstone of freedom.

Justice does not just apply in the social
arena alone but also means political and economic justice. Thus, we have retirement plans

of all sorts with tax benefits so that parents do not become dependent on their children in old age. In most of Asia and South and Central America and other emerging markets, including China, there is nothing as extensive as what we generously provide. Thus, children are always expected to care for their parents after their retirement.

We also have some of the finest and most advanced medical care in the world, mainly provided by enterprise and government. The hospitals for the poor in emerging market countries does not anywhere provide the quality of care comparable to what is available in America. The hospitals for the poor are provided mainly by governments. Given the political, economic, and social conditions mentioned earlier, it should come as no surprise that emerging market countries are heavily in debt and are chronically short of funding for social and medical welfare.

A selective tariff policy should not render us any less competitive in our export industries. In fact, if the world shifts from complete free trade to a selective moderate tariff policy, poverty in most countries, including the United States, would be reduced significantly. Social reasons for poverty in America stem mostly from alcoholism, drug addiction, mental illness, incapacity or unwillingness to gain an education, as well as many single women run families due to broken marriages or unwillingness to get married. Otherwise there should really be no economics-based reasons for there are more than sufficient economic theories and tools which are sources to help combat poverty. An example would be the coal mines which employ at wage levels and working conditions which can bring about ill health and poverty. The development of cleaner energy will enable us to eventually redeploy this labor force to better jobs.

The author does not believe that some moderate measure of selective tariffs will cause any significant loss of consumer purchasing power nor reduction in business profits. Business will improve with the fall in the levels of unemployment and encourage more business spending. I also believe world trade will be better balanced rather than the presently lopsided dominance by China's light manufacturing exports, the oil-rich countries, and India with its emerging strengths in high-tech processing service industries.

Presently the author does not perceive a better way to get us out of our present unemployment levels.

The references at the end reflect economic conditions up to the first quarter of 2010. [63] It shows that the economy got worse in 2009, and that in 2010 there have been some improvements in the first quarter. However, this may not mean much. References on travel and tourism show some minor improvements, as well. From the data, the author feels it gives more reason of the use of selective tariffs because the freeing of the Yuan, the currency of China, will not mean much. After all, China only has a small overall trade and current account surplus. This is so even though their trade surplus vis-a-vis the United States is substantial. Our trade deficit with China cannot be balanced by the freeing of the Yuan, in my opinion.

The major holders of U.S. Treasury Securities show that China has become one of the biggest holders of the U.S. currency over the shortest period of time. [64]

To conclude: investment spending through the stimulus package and a low interest rate policy will not, by themselves, take us out of recession. What are required are international trade policy changes as well as reductions in the budget deficits. Most monetary policy manifested by near-zero interest rates, in unguarded moments by the banking system could fuel another round of speculation. We also need labor-intensive jobs in manufacturing and office businesses.

Economics is both a science and an art. In the fashioning and shaping of economic policy, it is best that we utilize the finest theoretical tools presently available. However, the final policy formulated must always consider the nature and capabilities of our human and other resources, as well as our circumstances. Thus, if we, as a people, are given to speculation, the Fed and the banking system must be on guard so as not to trigger speculative fever through loose lending standards. It is not so much low interest rates per se that triggers speculation but rather loose lending standards. These and many other kinds of economic policy formulated in this manner will help ensure that indeed, in America, economic justice is for all.

[59] "With malice toward none; with charity for all; with firmness in the right, as God gives us to see the right, let us strive on to finish the work we are in; to bind up the nation's wounds." Abraham Lincoln, Second Inaugural Address, Saturday, March 4, 1865.

Value Added by Industry
[Billions of dollars]
Release date: May 25, 2010

Line		2004	2005	2006	2007	2008	2009
1	Gross domestic product	11,867.8	12,638.4	13,398.9	14,077.6	14,441.4	14,256.3
2	Private industries	10,360.1	11,052.5	11,731.1	12,315.2	12,588.0	12,323.8
3	Agriculture, forestry, fishing, and hunting	142.7	127.1	122.5	147.0	163.2	136.4
4	Farms	118.3	102.0	93.1	116.2	132.1	...
5	Forestry, fishing, and related activities	24.5	25.1	29.4	30.8	31.1	...
6	Mining	159.3	192.0	229.0	242.1	307.2	231.3
7	Oil and gas extraction	106.6	128.6	147.8	150.6	203.8	...
8	Mining, except oil and gas	31.0	36.3	40.7	43.8	48.8	...
9	Support activities for mining	21.7	27.2	40.5	47.7	54.7	...
10	Utilities	208.0	205.7	236.2	247.0	255.2	269.2
11	Construction	554.4	611.7	651.1	661.2	639.3	578.3
12	Manufacturing	1,482.7	1,568.0	1,651.5	1,708.6	1,669.6	1,568.6
13	Durable goods	822.0	877.6	923.1	947.0	923.4	846.8
14	Wood products	31.7	33.0	30.2	28.5	26.8	...
15	Nonmetallic mineral products	42.7	45.3	45.4	45.6	40.5	...
16	Primary metals	52.2	53.7	59.7	60.0	58.5	...
17	Fabricated metal products	112.7	120.4	125.6	135.9	135.7	...
18	Machinery	100.4	109.5	116.6	122.9	124.0	...
19	Computer and electronic products	159.6	183.3	200.0	197.7	195.2	...
20	Electrical equipment, appliances, and components	38.9	39.9	45.6	45.9	50.3	...
21	Motor vehicles, bodies and trailers, and parts	117.6	112.6	107.6	104.6	89.0	...
22	Other transportation equipment	67.2	76.0	81.5	93.6	94.0	...
23	Furniture and related products	31.1	34.3	36.6	33.3	30.2	...
24	Miscellaneous manufacturing	67.9	69.6	74.5	79.2	79.2	...
25	Nondurable goods	660.6	690.4	728.4	761.6	746.2	721.8
26	Food and beverage and tobacco products	168.9	172.1	181.4	184.8	189.5	...
27	Textile mills and textile product mills	26.8	23.5	21.2	21.6	16.9	...
28	Apparel and leather and allied products	16.4	16.0	15.5	15.0	14.2	...
29	Paper products	54.2	53.8	59.3	58.9	59.7	...
30	Printing and related support activities	37.0	37.5	37.9	38.7	37.1	...
31	Petroleum and coal products	106.3	139.3	140.0	146.4	149.2	...
32	Chemical products	186.8	182.7	207.9	224.7	212.8	...
33	Plastics and rubber products	64.3	65.6	65.1	71.4	66.7	...
34	Wholesale trade	684.5	725.3	769.6	816.5	821.0	793.3
35	Retail trade	794.7	838.8	875.0	892.8	866.0	842.2
36	Transportation and warehousing	347.0	369.7	395.5	407.7	405.4	393.9
37	Air transportation	56.1	55.7	59.7	61.3	57.3	...
38	Rail transportation	24.3	27.0	30.6	31.8	32.1	...
39	Water transportation	8.7	9.3	12.4	13.8	14.1	...
40	Truck transportation	110.2	118.9	125.3	126.8	125.6	...
41	Transit and ground passenger transportation	20.9	21.2	22.6	23.2	23.2	...
42	Pipeline transportation	11.5	10.4	11.3	13.8	13.7	...
43	Other transportation and support activities	83.9	91.9	96.4	96.8	98.7	...
44	Warehousing and storage	31.4	35.3	37.2	40.3	40.7	...
45	Information	564.1	592.6	593.3	622.8	622.5	633.8
46	Publishing industries (includes software)	140.8	151.2	133.9	146.1	145.5	...
47	Motion picture and sound recording industries	56.3	56.3	59.6	62.2	61.1	...

Value dded by Industry
(Billions if Dollars)
Release Date: May 25, 2010

48	Broadcasting and telecommunications	289.0	311.4	317.6	345.8	344.6	...
49	Information and data processing services	78.0	73.6	82.1	68.7	71.3	...
50	**Finance, insurance, real estate, rental, and leasing**	**2,409.7**	**2,606.5**	**2,777.6**	**2,905.9**	**3,042.5**	**3,057.8**
51	**Finance and insurance**	**929.2**	**1,028.5**	**1,105.5**	**1,121.7**	**1,200.0**	**1,198.0**
52	Federal Reserve banks, credit intermediation, and related activities	433.3	470.7	483.5	483.0	486.3	...
53	Securities, commodity contracts, and investments	144.0	183.0	214.5	201.1	196.1	...
54	Insurance carriers and related activities	319.6	337.5	367.4	392.5	464.0	...
55	Funds, trusts, and other financial vehicles	32.4	37.3	40.2	45.1	53.6	...
56	**Real estate and rental and leasing**	**1,480.4**	**1,577.9**	**1,672.1**	**1,784.2**	**1,842.5**	**1,859.8**
57	Real estate	1,337.6	1,424.9	1,488.6	1,585.5	1,647.0	...
58	Rental and leasing services and lessors of intangible assets	142.8	153.1	183.4	198.7	195.5	...
59	**Professional and business services**	**1,346.8**	**1,461.8**	**1,571.4**	**1,697.0**	**1,747.9**	**1,723.9**
60	**Professional, scientific, and technical services**	**810.5**	**875.6**	**952.2**	**1,023.8**	**1,070.6**	**1,077.5**
61	Legal services	180.7	194.5	201.9	211.4	209.6	...
62	Computer systems design and related services	117.7	129.3	144.3	160.2	169.7	...
63	Miscellaneous professional, scientific, and technical services	512.1	551.8	606.0	652.3	691.3	...
64	**Management of companies and enterprises**	**203.1**	**217.7**	**234.3**	**255.0**	**260.6**	**252.0**
65	**Administrative and waste management services**	**333.2**	**368.5**	**385.0**	**418.1**	**416.7**	**394.4**
66	Administrative and support services	299.0	331.3	350.4	378.1	375.9	...
67	Waste management and remediation services	34.3	37.2	34.6	40.0	40.8	...
68	**Educational services, health care, and social assistance**	**906.4**	**953.4**	**1,015.2**	**1,076.6**	**1,137.3**	**1,188.8**
69	**Educational services**	**116.0**	**120.1**	**128.7**	**137.1**	**145.9**	**152.7**
70	**Health care and social assistance**	**790.4**	**833.3**	**886.5**	**939.5**	**991.5**	**1,036.1**
71	Ambulatory health care services	381.4	406.1	432.3	458.1	485.9	...
72	Hospitals and nursing and residential care facilities	341.2	354.4	377.7	399.5	419.2	...
73	Social assistance	67.8	72.8	76.4	82.0	86.3	...
74	**Arts, entertainment, recreation, accommodation, and food services**	**456.7**	**481.6**	**511.3**	**537.4**	**545.5**	**545.6**
75	**Arts, entertainment, and recreation**	**113.3**	**117.3**	**126.6**	**131.8**	**138.0**	**137.9**
76	Performing arts, spectator sports, museums, and related activities	62.2	63.8	68.1	73.5	74.9	...
77	Amusements, gambling, and recreation industries	51.1	53.5	58.4	58.4	63.1	...
78	**Accommodation and food services**	**343.4**	**364.3**	**384.7**	**405.6**	**407.4**	**407.7**
79	Accommodation	100.6	108.7	113.6	121.0	119.1	...
80	Food services and drinking places	242.8	255.6	271.1	284.6	288.3	...
81	**Other services, except government**	**303.0**	**318.5**	**332.0**	**352.6**	**365.5**	**360.6**
82	**Government**	**1,507.7**	**1,585.9**	**1,667.8**	**1,764.4**	**1,853.4**	**1,932.5**
83	**Federal**	**478.4**	**501.8**	**526.5**	**552.1**	**578.5**	**625.6**
84	General government	412.0	438.7	460.6	485.7	515.2	...
85	Government enterprises	66.4	63.1	65.9	66.3	63.3	...
86	**State and local**	**1,029.3**	**1,084.1**	**1,141.3**	**1,210.3**	**1,274.9**	**1,306.9**
87	General government	947.3	997.7	1,051.3	1,116.0	1,173.2	...
88	Government enterprises	81.9	86.4	90.0	94.3	101.7	...
89	**Addenda:**						
90	Private goods-producing industries [1]	2,339.2	2,498.8	2,654.1	2,758.9	2,779.3	2,514.6
91	Private services-producing industries [2]	8,020.9	8,553.7	9,077.0	9,556.3	9,808.7	9,809.2
92	Information-communications-technology-producing industries [3]	496.2	537.4	560.3	572.7	581.6	562.5

1. Consists of agriculture, forestry, fishing, and hunting; mining; construction; and manufacturing.
2. Consists of utilities; wholesale trade; retail trade; transportation and warehousing; information; finance, insurance, real estate, rental, and leasing; professional and business services; educational services, health care, and social assistance; arts, entertainment, recreation, accommodation, and food services; and other services, except government.
3. Consists of computer and electronic products; publishing industries (includes software); information and data processing services; and computer systems design and related services.

Value Added by Industry
(Billions of Dollars)
Release Date: May 25, 2919

MAJOR FOREIGN HOLDERS OF TREASURY SECURITIES
(in billions of dollars)
HOLDINGS 1/ AT END OF PERIOD

Country	Jun 2010	May 2010	Apr 2010	Mar 2010	Feb 2010	Jan 2010	Dec 2009	Nov 2009	Oct 2009	Sep 2009	Aug 2009	Jul 2009	Jun 2009
China, Mainland	843.7	867.7	900.2	895.2	877.5	889.0	894.8	929.0	938.3	938.3	936.5	939.9	915.8
Japan	803.6	786.7	795.5	784.9	768.5	765.4	765.7	754.3	742.9	747.9	727.5	720.9	708.2
United Kingdom 2/	362.2	350.0	321.2	279.0	233.5	208.3	180.3	155.5	108.1	126.8	104.3	97.1	90.8
Oil Exporters 3/	223.0	235.1	239.3	229.5	218.8	218.4	207.4	208.3	209.0	205.9	209.8	209.9	211.8
Carib Bnkng Ctrs 4/	165.2	165.5	153.4	148.4	144.6	143.8	128.5	123.5	114.4	116.9	125.3	138.8	135.5
Brazil	158.4	161.4	164.3	164.4	170.8	169.1	169.3	165.8	164.9	153.6	146.0	146.8	148.5
Hong Kong	141.0	145.7	151.8	150.9	152.4	146.6	148.7	142.1	137.8	128.0	120.5	111.1	95.7
Taiwan	128.6	126.2	126.9	124.8	121.4	119.6	116.5	115.4	115.6	115.1	112.9	114.4	114.0
Russia	123.4	126.8	113.1	120.1	120.2	124.2	141.8	151.4	145.9	145.1	144.9	141.3	143.3
Switzerland	100.1	84.4	80.0	78.8	81.8	84.4	89.7	89.6	85.3	82.7	82.0	81.9	85.7
Luxembourg	97.5	76.3	77.6	84.6	77.9	79.1	88.4	80.2	79.5	87.5	83.0	80.8	92.9
Canada	94.0	85.0	82.1	77.0	67.1	54.7	52.8	50.7	44.8	42.3	30.2	24.1	23.0
Germany	53.5	55.4	54.3	53.7	49.9	49.0	47.8	48.7	47.9	48.8	50.1	51.2	48.9
Singapore	50.5	40.6	42.4	45.5	42.6	41.3	39.2	37.5	36.3	39.4	43.1	43.4	41.9
Thailand	49.3	46.3	46.9	43.5	42.1	33.3	33.3	29.6	28.0	27.9	31.4	23.3	27.5
Ireland	48.3	48.0	45.7	43.3	38.7	39.2	43.6	43.1	42.6	37.0	40.8	42.9	50.6
Korea, South	38.7	37.8	38.7	40.1	39.8	39.7	40.3	40.2	42.3	39.9	39.8	38.7	37.4
India	36.4	29.3	31.0	32.0	31.6	32.7	32.5	34.5	35.8	38.8	41.5	41.8	42.2
France	35.2	36.4	38.8	38.7	32.5	35.9	30.5	40.4	29.1	25.0	28.0	17.5	18.9
Mexico	33.0	34.1	33.1	36.1	33.9	34.4	36.8	31.9	26.5	27.8	33.2	33.4	35.2
Egypt	29.4	28.0	21.1	21.4	21.7	19.4	18.9	19.4	14.3	14.9	14.5	12.7	11.5
Turkey	25.5	27.6	27.9	28.7	27.3	27.5	28.1	29.4	30.3	28.1	28.5	27.1	27.3
Poland	23.2	23.4	24.6	23.4	23.6	22.3	22.9	21.9	21.9	21.5	21.3	20.9	20.5
Italy	20.1	20.8	20.3	20.5	20.9	21.3	21.1	21.6	21.6	20.0	19.3	19.8	19.1
Israel	18.4	20.1	19.9	22.0	18.9	16.8	13.8	15.1	14.5	14.9	16.2	15.5	16.6
Netherlands	17.3	17.6	19.6	19.2	20.4	20.7	20.4	21.0	20.5	22.0	22.0	22.2	19.6
Belgium	17.2	17.6	18.5	17.1	17.0	17.4	17.3	17.4	16.9	17.2	17.7	17.8	17.9
Colombia	17.0	15.7	15.7	16.2	16.0	16.0	17.3	17.2	18.3	18.3	17.9	16.4	13.3
Sweden	16.5	13.4	15.3	16.3	16.0	15.7	15.2	15.5	15.3	14.4	12.7	12.5	12.5
Norway	16.1	15.2	15.0	14.6	13.6	12.3	12.1	8.5	7.3	7.6	7.1	11.3	11.1
Australia	14.5	14.1	17.9	14.4	14.4	15.4	16.3	13.7	12.8	12.3	12.5	12.1	12.5
Philippines	14.3	14.4	15.0	14.6	12.5	11.3	11.7	11.7	11.4	11.4	11.9	10.9	11.2
Denmark	13.0	12.8	9.7	9.6	9.8	8.9	8.5	7.8	7.7	7.7	7.1	5.3	5.5	5.3
Chile	12.2	12.0	12.0	11.9	12.3	12.5	12.4	12.1	12.4	12.8	12.9	13.4	14.2
Malaysia	11.1	10.5	10.9	11.0	10.9	11.0	11.7	11.8	11.7	11.7	11.9	12.5	12.4
All Other	158.1	161.7	158.4	153.7	152.2	152.2	155.9	159.2	163.3	164.6	168.5	169.9	168.2
Grand Total	4009.2	3963.6	3957.9	3885.0	3752.3	3708.0	3691.7	3675.0	3576.1	3575.5	3531.1	3505.8	3460.8
Of which:													
For. Official	2696.7	2697.2	2721.6	2709.4	2677.1	2681.1	2706.3	2734.3	2714.5	2699.2	2689.8	2675.9	2625.5
Treasury Bills	460.7	473.4	505.0	507.3	503.4	508.5	534.3	586.6	598.0	597.7	607.3	606.6	571.9
T-Bonds & Notes	2235.9	2223.8	2216.6	2202.0	2173.8	2172.6	2172.0	2147.7	2116.5	2101.5	2082.5	2069.3	2053.6

Department of the Treasury/Federal Reserve Board
August 16, 2010

1/ Estimated foreign holdings of U.S. Treasury marketable and non-marketable bills, bonds, and notes
reported under the Treasury International Capital (TIC) reporting system are based on annual
Surveys of Foreign Holdings of U.S. Securities and on monthly data.
2/ United Kingdom includes Channel Islands and Isle of Man.
3/ Oil exporters include Ecuador, Venezuela, Indonesia, Bahrain, Iran, Iraq, Kuwait, Oman, Qatar,
Saudi Arabia, the United Arab Emirates, Algeria, Gabon, Libya, and Nigeria.
4/ Caribbean Banking Centers include Bahamas, Bermuda, Cayman Islands, Netherlands Antilles and Panama.
Beginning with new series for June 2006, also includes British Virgin Islands.

Major Holders of Treasury Securities
(In Billions of Dollars)
Holdings1. At End of Period

(60) U.S. International Trade in Goods and Services, U.S. Census Bureau, Foreign Trade Statistics 2009

(61) Top 15 International Trading Partners of the U.S.A. (2009), U.S. Census Bureau, Foreign Trade Statistics

(62) The Last Resort of Kings and Common Men" refers to the act of declaring war.

(63) Major Holders of U.S. Treasury Securities, Federal Reserve Board Statistics

ABOUT THE AUTHOR

B.S.B.A. '65 (Major Management) University of the East, Manila, Philippines

B.Ecs. '69 (Major Accounting, Minor Political Science) University of Sydney, Australia

Books Published: (Manila, Philippined)

"How to Invest 50 Pesos a Month into a Fortune" (Published 1976)

"High Finance for any Business" (1977)

"The Art of Making Money in the Stockmarket" (1978)

Experience: (Manila, Philippines)

Worked in Family owned business in fabrication and assembly of sheet metal products mainly Truck & Bus Bodies

(Sydney< Australia)

Worked as an auditor then w/investment bankers as an investment analyst, then as a stockbroker

(Manila, Philippines)

Conducted seminars in Economics, Finance, Accounting, Marketing & Corporate Strategy

Migrated to America in 2003 and has lived in Las Vegas, Nv. Since 2004